MONDO

Also available from Mondo :

THE MAN WHO COULD NOT KILL ENOUGH
The Secret Murders of Jeffrey Dahmer

THE SECRET LIFE OF A SATANIST
The Authorised Biography of Anton LaVey

ZODIAC
The True Story of America's Most Bizarre Mass Murderer

The True Story of California's
Vampire Killer

the

DRACULA KILLER

Lt. Ray Biondi & Walt Hecox

MONDO

THE DRACULA KILLER
ISBN 1 85286 455 9

Published by
Mondo
An imprint of Titan Books Ltd
19 Valentine Place
London SE1 8QH

First Mondo Edition November 1992
10 9 8 7 6 5 4 3 2 1

British edition by arrangement
with Pocket Books, USA.

Note to the reader: Some of the names in this book have been changed.

Printed and bound in Great Britain by Cox and Wyman Ltd, Reading,
Berkshire.

Authors' Note

This book is dedicated to Ambrose Griffin, Teresa Wallin, Daniel Meredith, Evelyn Miroth, Jason Miroth, David Ferreira and their families.

I am ever mindful of the sufferings of the survivors caused by the loss of a loved one from senseless violence. Throughout the research and writing of this book, the thought foremost in my mind was the effect this book will have on the families of those killed by Richard Chase. It is not my intent to rekindle those horrible memories of over a decade ago. While I know the victims will always be remembered by their families, I hope time has eased the void left in each family.

This case is often lectured about and documented in textbooks and other training material as a classic case in psychological profiling. Usually the facts are massaged or omitted to illustrate how the case was solved by the sole use of a psychological profile. I believe in any training that may provide another tool to the homicide detective. However, the practical use of this training is very limited. The danger in the belief of psychological profiling is that it may cause an investigation to focus away from the true killer. The intention of this book is to correct the misconception that complex murder cases are solved solely on the basis of a psychological profile.

Ray Biondi
April, 1992

Foreword

"The world of the homicide investigator is permeated by the sudden, senseless, and violent deaths which often traumatize entire communities. Ironically, many of these murderous scenarios begin to blend into identifiable patterns and motives for violent behavior. It is the recognition of these patterns and motives that enables professional homicide detectives to effectively investigate murder cases, as well as psychologically cope with the reality of violent death."

—V.J.G.

So what happens when within a short span of time there are a series of brutal murders involving sexual mutilation and other atrocities so grotesque and violent that there is absolutely no frame of reference nor rationale to explain their occurrence?
The Dracula Killer vividly presents this scenario to the reader in a series of killings and bizarre lust murders which terrorized the people of Sacramento County, California, and thoroughly perplexed the law enforcement community. This is the story of Richard Trenton Chase, who like a real-life *vampire* drank the blood of his victims.

FOREWORD

It should be noted that the F.B.I.'s Behavioral Science Unit — recently made famous by the popular book and movie *The Silence of the Lambs* — has presented their assessment of portions of this case to law enforcement groups across the United States and Canada. In addition, the F.B.I. has also cited segments of the Chase case in their research relative to the phenomenon of serial killers. *In fact, this case is the classic example of the Disorganized Serial Killer,* (with Ted Bundy being the most accurate example of an Organized Serial Killer).

Now, for the very first time, the facts of this bizarre case are presented to the reader by Detective Lieutenant Ray Biondi, a veteran homicide commander and expert on serial killers, and Walt Hecox, an established journalist.

It was Detective Lieutenant Ray Biondi who actually led the intensive manhunt for Richard Chase, the murderer who was the very personification of the term "blood thirsty killer." I doubt you'll soon forget this case of *The Dracula Killer.*

VERNON J. GEBERTH, Lieutenant-Commander (Ret.)

Commanding Officer, Bronx Homicide Task Force N.Y.P.D.

Author of *PRACTICAL HOMICIDE INVESTIGATION: Tactics, Procedures, and Forensic Techniques. Second Edition, 1990.*

The Disorganized Offender

The disorganized offender is generally a loner type who usually is not married and lives either alone or with a relative in close proximity to the crime scene. He experiences difficulty in negotiating interpersonal relationships and is described as socially inadequate.

He acts impulsively under stress and will usually select a victim from his own geographic area. Generally, he will avoid people and can be described as sexually incompetent, i.e., without any meaningful sexual relationships. He uses a "blitz style" of attack, which catches the victim off guard. This spontaneous action, in which the offender suddenly "acts out" his fantasy, does not allow for a conscious plan or even the thought of being detected, which is why the crime scene will be disorganized.

Vernon J. Geberth,
Practical Homicide Investigation: Tactics, Procedures and Forensic Techniques
(Elsevier Science Publishing Co., Inc. 1990)

Prologue

Pyramid Lake, Nevada

August 3, 1977

Pyramid Lake gleamed a startling sapphire in the sunlight, basking in the warmth of summer. This piece of Nevada landscape, more desolate than most in the state that embraces sagebrush as its official flower, was no place for a stranded man on foot to be wandering.

Such a mercy mission was what Bureau of Indian Affairs Officer Charles O'Brien thought he had undertaken after being advised by radio that a vehicle had apparently been abandoned by a lone man after it was driven into the sand near the shore of the lake.

Pyramid Lake and the land surrounding it are part of the vast Walker River Reservation, populated primarily by members of the Piute Indian tribe.

O'Brien, soon joined by other BIA officers and Piute tribal officers, located a silver 1966 Ford Ranchero with expired Florida license tags sunk up to its hubcaps in the desert sands.

Opening the driver's door, O'Brien peered inside the cab. On the seat were two weapons: a 30/30 lever-action Marlin rifle loaded with four rounds and a .22 semiautomatic rifle, its clip loaded with two rounds. Both rifles were stained with what appeared to be blood.

A pile of men's clothing and a pair of bloody tennis shoes had been deposited on the seat in a heap, as if someone had undressed in a hurry.

But nothing so far had prepared O'Brien for what he found in a white plastic bucket on the floor: a raw, perfectly shaped liver, sitting in a pool of fresh blood! It was a big hunk of meat. O'Brien realized with a shudder that one of the few living things big enough to be equipped with this sizable organ was a human being.

These reservation cops knew about busting drunken drivers, breaking up bar fights, and finding lost hikers. But what in God's name did they have on their hands?

Using high-powered field glasses to scan the horizon, they eventually spotted a man sitting about a half mile to the south. He was perched, stark naked, on a rocky projection that rose well over the high chaparral.

When he saw the officers moving in his direction he quickly slid down off the rocks and raced like a frightened jackrabbit across the white-hot sands—in the opposite direction, away from them. The chase was on.

Two tribal officers in a four-wheel drive caught up with their quarry in no time, took him into custody, and returned to the pickup.

Blood was smeared across his torso and face like Indian war paint. The man was filthy. His hair was long and matted; his skin had the waxen hue that people who seldom see the sun develop. An inch shy of six feet, he was unusually thin, weighing perhaps all of 145 pounds.

Responding to O'Brien's questions, the subject identified himself as Richard Trenton Chase, age twenty-seven, of Sacramento, California. He confirmed the pickup was his.

"Where did the blood come from?" O'Brien asked.

"It's seeping—from me." The voice was soft, somewhat high-pitched. His eyes darted back and forth.

"What were you doing when the truck got stuck?"

"Just lookin' around."

O'Brien had the man put his clothes on. As he did, the officer noted that the suspect had crusted blood under his armpits, in his whiskers, and even in his ears.

"Now Richard, where did the blood come from?"

"I shot a deer."

"Where?"

"In Colorado."

"When?"

"Sometime in May."

Obviously, this blood was *not* three months old.

O'Brien informed Chase he was going to be taken to the tribal ranger station for further questioning. The suspect became unruly at that point and had to be physically restrained and placed in the vehicle.

Chase was given his Miranda warning and arrested for a variety of federal gun law violations. Soon he was en route to Washoe County jail in Reno.

Four days later, laboratory tests on the blood and liver revealed them to be from a cow. As a result, all charges were dropped against Richard Trenton Chase. He was released, and he immediately headed home. To Sacramento County.

My beat.

1

December 29, 1977

When the phone rang at 9 P.M. I groaned. I didn't want to answer it, but I did. On the second ring.

"Biondi, Homicide," I said, forgetting for a moment that I was home.

I was then an inspector, with fifteen years under my belt, and had been chief of Homicide for the Sacramento County Sheriff's Department for less than two years.

Despite the time off I had just spent with my family over Christmas, I was bushed.

Maybe, I'd reflected earlier in the day, I was dragging tail *because* of my days off. My wife Carol and I had five boys ranging from five to fourteen years of age, and they were experts in keeping Mom and Dad on the run.

Sacramento County was closing out 1977 with a bang, and that was the right word for it. Unfortunately, it wasn't going to get better anytime soon. Too many people in my jurisdiction were having their lives end unnaturally, with deliberateness and enthusiasm. Our citizens, it seemed, were dying around us at an alarming rate.

On the phone was the duty dispatcher, who was in constant touch by radio with our units patrolling the approximately nine hundred square miles of unincorporated area that encircled the state capital. She reported, in the emotionless, monotone delivery of police dispatchers everywhere, a shooting at 3734 Robertson Avenue. Though not yet a homicide, it sounded as if it had the makings of one.

Hanging up, I quickly decided to assign the case to Sergeant Don Habecker and Detective Fred Homen, and I made the appropriate phone calls.

Habecker had been in Homicide a year or so longer than I had, and he had become my right hand. Quiet, low-key, unflappable under fire, he could be counted on to supervise the investigation at the crime scene. A family man, he had all boys, too—three of them— and we were always trading stories about our sons' latest rounds of mischief.

Homen, a trim statue of a man with curly dark hair, exuded genuine congeniality from every pore and had the well-deserved moniker of "Friendly Fred." Not surprisingly, he was the consummate organizer of law enforcement social functions. But in house he had another nickname. Time and again, when any of us walked away from our disheveled desks in Homicide for any length of time, we would return to a newly organized desktop—irrefutable proof that "Mr. Clean" had struck again. Homen, characteristically, had made an art out of the careful collection and labeling of evidentiary minutiae at the scene, always the first step toward finding the perpetrator.

When the two detectives arrived at the modest tract house on the east side of town they directed patrol units to seal off the area to keep the curious at bay.

Then Habecker and Homen went to work.

When Habecker arrived at the hospital later that night he was told that Ambrose Griffin had just expired in the emergency room.

The ambulance had been followed to the hospital by the victim's wife and two sons, and their wives. They were now in a room at the hospital with a Catholic priest, Habecker was told by a family friend. Would it be all right if he waited until tomorrow to question them?

Habecker didn't push. The grieving family deserved privacy. Of course, had he any reason to suspect a relative, Habecker wouldn't have been so thoughtful. But from all indications and reports at the scene, the killing appeared to be what we in the business call a "drive-by."

He spoke to Carol Griffin and her sons the next morning in the living room at the house on Robertson Avenue. The more she thought about it, she *did* remember having heard two popping noises, she told Habecker. They hadn't meant anything at the time. What had concerned her greatly and occupied all of her attention at that moment had been the frightful sound of her husband yelling.

He stopped almost as soon as he started, she

explained, pushing a wadded tissue to the corner of one reddened eye. Then he turned toward where she was standing in the doorway of their home and, with no further sound, crumpled to the ground.

Carol Griffin remembered screaming and running toward her husband. As she did she shouted over her shoulder to their two sons, who were in the house. "Call for help! Your father had a heart attack!" She noticed the trunk of the car was still open. The thought crossed her mind that her husband must not have reached the car before the attack struck him down. When they had arrived home from their shopping trip and parked in the driveway a few moments earlier, he had handed her the keys and asked her to open the trunk. She had done so and had taken a sack of potatoes into the house with her. Ambrose had followed with two sacks of groceries. He was returning for the last two bags in the trunk when it happened.

Habecker knew, from interviewing witnesses at the scene, that Carol Griffin had knelt beside her stricken husband, sobbing to neighbors about his being "just the right age for a heart attack."

Not until the fire department paramedics arrived did she learned that a heart attack had nothing to do with her husband's condition.

As soon as I was briefed on the details I worried that the shooting on Robertson Avenue—in what was referred to as Sacramento's East Area—was going to be a tough one to solve. Most murders, senseless as they may be, do have some sort of pattern and visible motive, whether it's robbery, anger, or jealousy. So far, this one lacked such order.

Ambrose Griffin, an engineer for the Federal Bureau of Land Management in Sacramento, was fifty-one years old. According to his family, he was an even-tempered man with no known enemies. Later, Griffin's fellow employees in the office where he worked agreed. He was a upper-middle-class civil servant who had, like thousands of others, settled in one of the sprawling tree-studded subdivisions that had sprouted after World War II in the suburbs of Sacramento. He and Carol had raised a family there and planned to stay at least until they reached retirement age. They loved the home on the oversized lot that backed onto a meandering creek bed.

The picture we were getting of our victim would have placed him comfortably on a Norman Rockwell magazine cover. His was a loving, supportive family that gathered at the Griffin home for holidays. He was Mr. Regular Guy whose clothes stamped him Middle America, from the white T-shirts to the sleeveless sweater from Ward's to the Pendleton-plaid shirts he wore on evenings at home.

But someone had shot him down as he walked, supremely confident of his safety—as well he should have been—from his house to his parked car. My God, he was killed in his own yard!

Soon the two Griffin sons produced what they hoped would be a clue to their father's death. Bob Griffin, the younger son of the murdered man, called Homicide to say that his brother Rick had seen a man carrying a rifle near the Griffin home. They were outraged and angry when they spotted the man with the gun so soon after their father was shot. They followed the man to a house on a nearby street, then called us.

We went out and talked to the man. His rifle, a 30/30-caliber hunting rifle, was not our murder weapon. Ambrose Griffin had been shot with a smaller .22-caliber weapon. In addition, the man had an alibi: He had been working at a gas station when the shooting on Robertson Avenue occurred. He was not our man.

As we always do, whenever we are able to after a homicide, we packed a lot of work into the next twenty-four sleepless hours. Sheriff's deputies or detectives talked to everyone residing within two blocks of the shooting scene. Then the questioning spread to adjoining streets.

We found a lot of people who had heard what they believed, well after the fact, to have been the fatal shots the evening Ambrose Griffin was shot. The trouble was that they didn't think them to be gunshots at the time. In fact, no one on the block had taken the trouble to look outside his house until the emergency vehicles began to arrive.

Worse yet, no one who lived in the area was particularly disturbed by gunfire. It was far too common there. The creek bed that bordered most of the property was perfectly suited to what gun enthusiasts call "plinking"—target shooting at cans. As close as we could tell, a small battle could have been fought in that creek bed without any of the neighbors reporting gunshots.

During the week following the murder of Ambrose Griffin we met a wide variety of people who believed they knew something about the shooting. Some told us flat out they knew who killed the engineer. None of them was right. They knew someone who owned a gun and had a bad reputation or someone they didn't like. Reports like that are inclined to make the job of catching a killer more tedious and even worse, waste a lot of investigative efforts. Yet some of these witnesses could have had pertinent information. It's chancy to try to judge their validity until the facts have been carefully studied. But working against such deliberation is the reality that speed during a homicide investigation can often be the difference between apprehending and not apprehending the suspect.

Clues reached us in bits and pieces.

At 10 A.M. on the day after the murder, with the help of the light of day, two spent shell casings were found on the pavement near the Griffin's house by a TV news crew sent to photograph the crime scene. One of the cartridge casings was crushed when it had been either run over by a car or perhaps stepped on in the darkness. The other was unharmed. Both were .22 casings. We went back to the scene immediately and recovered the new evidence.

The other detectives joined in my embarrassment that a TV crew would find important evidence. Since homicide detectives rarely save lives, we usually park a distance away and walk to the crime scene, arriving cautiously so as not to disrupt the scene. The difference is that we think in terms of hours (to search thoroughly for evidence), while emergency personnel such as paramedics and patrol officers think of terms of the seconds and minutes they have to revive an unconscious person or catch an armed suspect on the scene. Any number of vehicles might have parked on the casings the night before. I sincerely hoped it hadn't been a detective's car. Admittedly, I winced that evening when the TV station reported its "exclusive." The lesson was not forgotten.

Detectives measured the distance from the point where the two shell casings were found to the place where Griffin's body fell after being shot. One was 71'8" away, the other 83' from where Griffin fell. Booked as evidence, the casings, according to the crime lab, "may have been fired by the same gun" that had killed the engineer. Unfortunately, lacking the gun itself and unable to perform any test firings, that was as close to a match as science could get us. (Bullets fired from the same gun are easier to match than a bullet to a casing.)

Hard as it was to find real evidence, theories were easy to find, coming from almost all quarters. Our first thought, of course, was that someone wanted Griffin dead. In other words, he had an enemy. That might still be the case, though based on our interviews with his family and friends, it seemed unlikely. The second possibility, which loomed as more likely, was that this was a "thrill" crime, and Griffin was simply a random target. Earlier in the year we had solved a murder that occurred when three escapees from a juvenile facility came across a fisherman sleeping in his truck. The juveniles shot the fisherman as he slept for no apparent reason. (They hadn't even stolen his truck.) Griffin, like the fisherman, could have been a victim simply because someone liked to kill. Such a crime, with the victim in the wrong place at the wrong time, was the most difficult to solve, bar none. (A decade later I testified in Carson City, Nevada, where the shooter of the fisherman went on trial for another murder. He was convicted and received the death penalty.)

We felt our best hope now was to identify and locate a suspicious vehicle that had been reported by several neighbors as driving slowly down the block around the time of the shooting. They couldn't agree, though, whether it was a Ford or Chevy or Pontiac. One woman even thought it was a small pickup.

The plan was to continue canvasing until reliable sightings of the vehicle could be developed. The next step would be to publicize the vehicle in the hope of getting the "magic" phone call from someone who could identify the driver and/or occupants.

December 30, 1977

On the afternoon after the Griffin murder a twelve-year-old boy was riding his bicycle. Like a lot of boys just entering their teens, he was interested in racy automobiles. His favorite was a Pontiac Trans Am.

He was riding his bike in front of Long's Drugs on Marconi Avenue, just blocks from the Griffin neighborhood, when he happened to notice a brown Trans Am traveling in the opposite direction. While he watched the car, the driver took his hands off the steering wheel, pulled a gun, pointed it out the window, and shot at the boy.

At the crack of the gun the boy jumped from his

bike and fell. He was not hit, only shaken by the incident.

He told detectives later that day that the weapon fired at him was a short, snub-nosed handgun of some type. He described the driver as being in his early twenties, with brown hair. Not much to go on.

The seventh grader's mother told us her son was a "good boy and exceptional student" not given to lying or indulging in fantasies. His story, coupled with the fact that a tan or brown Trans Am had been seen by some witnesses on Robertson Avenue, impressed us.

Aware that the boy's subconscious might contain more descriptive details of his assailant, we sought permission from his parents to have him hypnotized. They granted their approval with the provision that one of them be present during the session. I wouldn't have had it any other way.

Law enforcement is always looking for an added edge, a new and better way to get the job done. In the 1970s hypnosis was the latest innovation. Courts soon ruled in appeals brought by defense counsels that hypnotized witnesses were subject to subtle suggestions by the police, and thus the information obtained under hypnosis was unreliable. Eventually the courts reversed themselves and allowed information received under hypnosis when strict guidelines were followed. In part, sessions had to be videotaped, witnessed, and conducted by a trained professional with the proper credentials. (Prior to these guidelines we were doing most of these things already, though some other departments were much looser in their practices. Today, in the 1990s, we have better training in interrogation and cognitive interviewing, and as a result hypnosis is seldom used anymore. Some things stick, some don't.)

Two days later we arranged for Leroy Wolter, a Ph.D. hypnotist, to conduct a session with the boy in the video room on the second floor of the Sheriff's Department. The twelve-year-old proved to be a good subject and gave some further details about the car and its lone occupant. He also remembered the license plate number, 219EEP.

We ran the license number the boy recalled, plus ninety numbers similar to it (e.g., 219EPP, 291EEP), through the Department of Motors Vehicles computer. The search failed to produce a single Trans Am or any registered owners in the Sacramento area. There were two Pontiacs registered to numbers faintly resembling those produced by the boy under hypnosis, but they were not brown and were different models.

This typifies the kind of information that surfaces early in murder investigations. Such incidents as the boy being shot at do require checking out, but often they take us nowhere. In this case, the Trans Am shooting suspect and his snub-nosed gun were not connected to our case.

January 9, 1978

On this day we got our first big break. It came in a phone call from the crime lab. But allow me to back up a moment.

Our break had come about, typically, from hard, joyless work of the variety you don't often see on a TV detective show. (Though now that I've said that, I do recall Joe Friday wearing out a lot of shoe leather on the job, and that *is* realistic.)

After days canvasing in the Griffin neighborhood and questioning residents for more information, Sergeant Habecker and Detective Homen had returned to the office and begun the unenviable task of going through reports taken by patrol units in that area in the days before the fatal shooting, hoping to find something, *anything*.

They came across a routine report filed by a patrol officer on December 27, 1977. On that date a woman who lived on Lynn Avenue, a few blocks away from the Griffin house, reported a shot fired into her home.

Dorothy Polenske had been in her kitchen at 6:30 P.M. doing the dinner dishes when she heard a sharp, explosive noise. At almost the same instant the kitchen window broke, and she felt something hot pass through her hair, which she wore in a thick bun on the top of her head. She ran her finger through her hair but didn't find anything. It had been a bullet, that she was sure. But there was nothing to find in the kitchen other than the broken window glass.

There was not much the responding patrolman had been able to do but take her report and file it away under "random shooting—no injuries."

The Polenske shooting had occurred two days before the Griffin murder.

Habecker and Homen agreed they should interview her.

Dorothy Polenske was surprised to see the two

detectives at her door. It impressed her that the department was still so concerned. She had, of course, heard about the shooting a few blocks away. "Do you think there's any connection?" she asked anxiously.

"We don't know, ma'am," one of the detectives responded. "But we'd like to look in your kitchen, if you don't mind."

They went through the kitchen slowly, carefully checking every nook and cranny, as if they had nothing better to do.

About half an hour after taking off their coats and rolling up their sleeves they found what they were looking for in a cupboard filled with crockery. Though not a single dish or cup had been broken, they found what appeared to be a .22-caliber slug embedded in a shelf. They carefully dug it out and brought it back with them. And that very afternoon they turned it in to the crime lab.

And now criminalist Alan Gilmore was on the phone telling me the results of their tests.

"The recovered bullet was fired," Gilmore reported with a note of satisfaction, "from the same gun as the projectile that killed Ambrose Griffin."

"Would you say that again?"

He did, and I had heard right the first time.

The gun match made from the two shooting incidents suggested what we feared the most: This was the work of a random shooter.

The woman had been luckier than Ambrose Griffin, but there hadn't been any motive to kill her either. What we were dealing with, unquestionably, was a warped mind that had decided to start shooting at people.

I didn't think the shooter would stop on his own. These creeps seldom do. Often their crimes became more audacious, and progressively more deadly.

We had to get him fast, before he struck again.

2

January 11, 1978

For Dawn Larson it was moving day.

The attractive young woman had lived in a large apartment complex on Watt Avenue—in a congested East Area neighborhood—since the summer before.

Taking a break from tedium of packing, she had gone to check her mail. It was at the long wall of mailboxes that her neighbor from Apartment 15 cornered her.

He was, she had long thought, a very odd man. He was obviously lonely, as there were few visitors to his apartment. He wasn't at all like the other residents of the complex, who would exchange a smile or friendly word. Though she had seen the man almost daily in the six months they had been neighbors and always made it a point to greet him, her salutations had never been returned. He just hurried through the complex —usually coming and going at night—as if he had pressing business waiting.

Now and then, very late at night, she had heard the sound of something like firecrackers coming from his unit. She never knocked on his door, or asked him about it, or reported him. She was, after all, a good neighbor.

During the summer she had seen him on three separate occasions carrying animals into his apartment. Once she had seen him climb out of his car—an older pickup-style Ford Ranchero with a sign that said, "I'd Rather Be Flying" where the front license plate belonged—carrying a puppy. Soon after, she'd seen him entering his apartment with a second dog. Another time he had a cat. The complex had a no-pets rule, but then, she'd never seen the animals again. She had wondered, sometimes, about those animals.

Suddenly Richard Chase appeared at the mailboxes. He was out of cigarettes, he muttered unhappily. For the first time since they had lived next door to each other she knew for certain that her neighbor could talk.

"Do you have a cigarette?" he asked abruptly.

Smiling, she produced a package of cigarettes and gave him one. Then she started walking away.

A surprisingly strong hand stopped her. It gripped her shoulder tightly, hurting her. She turned, and the young man was staring boldly at her, as if really noticing her for the first time. Somehow his eyes were smoldering.

"Any more?" he demanded.

She gave him the entire pack.

He turned and left.

Dawn Larson had the strange feeling, as she returned to her packing with renewed enthusiasm, that she was moving out of the Watt Avenue complex just in time.

January 23, 1978

It was a clear and cold day in Sacramento.

At 2909 Burnece Street, one block east of the big apartment complex on Watt Avenue, a housewife glanced into her backyard shortly before 10 A.M. and saw an unkempt young man strolling toward her house. She watched in terror as he tried the patio door. Oh, dear God, she thought. Did we remember to lock it?

Immobilized by her terror, Jeanne Layton watched while the man tested the door, found it locked, then tried a kitchen window. When he roamed around a corner and out of sight she found the will to move with him. The windows were all locked. He headed once more toward the patio.

She returned to the kitchen. They met there, face to face through a pane of glass, at the window above the sink. She would never forget that moment. Not ever.

The face of the man looking at her was not wholly wild. It was only a day from a decent shave, and the dark hair was mussed. But what was beyond belief was that the intruder's face, just inches from her own, did not show one iota of emotion. Not surprise, or fear, or embarrassment. He just looked at her the way a man might look at a car he was contemplating buying, with complete inscrutability.

Eventually he muttered something that sounded like "excuse me." He paused on the patio for a moment, lit a cigarette, and walked away.

Layton, rubbery-legged, sat at her kitchen table. Her first impulse was to call the police. But then, as she composed herself, she began to reconsider. What had the guy done? He'd walked through her yard and tried the doors, but then excused himself and left. Maybe he was looking for another house. Did he have a friend or relative on the block?

Thirty minutes later

The residents of 2929 Burnece returned from a short shopping trip. As Robert and Barbara Edwards headed from their car to the door with groceries a noise from the supposedly empty house stopped them from putting the key in the lock. They looked at each other. Someone was inside their house.

In another moment they heard the sound of running footsteps inside. Whoever was inside was headed toward the rear of the house. They heard a window slam in a back room.

Seconds later a dirty young man rounded the corner of the house and came eye-to-eye with them.

"Hold it!" Robert Edwards shouted.

But the stranger had no intention of standing still. He plunged past them, ran out to the sidewalk, and sprinted up the block.

Edwards chased the burglar.

They headed in the direction of Watt Avenue.

For a few blocks the intruder stayed on the sidewalks. The streets in that area were pretty well deserted at that hour on a Monday morning. Briefly the homeowner gained ground, and the distance between the running men narrowed. Then the fugitive cut sharply to the right, ran across a lawn separating two houses, and headed for a fence.

"Stop!" Edwards shouted as the younger man topped the stained redwood boards.

The fugitive felt compelled to answer. "I'm just taking a shortcut," he yelled back, then he disappeared.

Edwards, red-faced and panting, returned to his home.

At the house on Burnece Street, several uniformed deputies had responded to his wife's call for help. A couple of detectives who had been cruising nearby and heard the dispatcher were also present.

As for the house, it was a complete shambles. The burglar had been both thorough and disgusting.

Deputies found the window in a back room where the intruder had both entered and left the house. Footprints in the soft earth beneath the window marked his progress. Eventually, the officers told the homeowner, technicians would want to photograph the prints and make plaster casts of the impressions they had left.

In the short time the intruder had been inside he had found all the rings in the house and put them in a single jewelry box. A couple of pairs of binoculars, a cassette tape player, a decorative dagger, and a stethoscope had all been placed in a cloth bag. Some clothing had been strewn across beds and floors after being pulled from closets and bureau drawers. But the intruder, obviously surprised by the arrival of the homeowners, had left without the items he collected so carefully.

Before much time had passed, deputies, canvasing the area in time-honored fashion, found Jeanne Layton, who had seen the young man in her yard but not reported it.

As the detectives followed the intruder's path through the house on Burnece Street they discovered he was more untidy than most burglars. Although he appeared to be thorough and methodical, his trail somehow looked as though it had been left by an amateur. And not just by someone interested in stealing items that could be sold, but by someone who had strange, perverted desires.

The burglar had opened a chest of drawers in a spare bedroom and urinated on the fresh, carefully folded baby clothes stored there. In the children's room he had defecated in the middle of a child's bed.

An hour later

Shortly before noon that day a woman in her late twenties was shopping at the Pantry Market, an upscale grocery market in the Town and Country Village shopping center on El Paseo Lane, not far from Watt Avenue.

As Nancy Holden pushed her cart down one aisle she noticed a filthy man approaching from the opposite direction. He appeared confused, as if loaded on drugs.

She quickly looked away to avoid eye contact, as most intelligent women living in a big city learn to do as a matter of survival.

"Were you on the motorcycle when Kurt was killed?"

His off-the-wall question was targeted at her, she realized with a start, as they were alone in the aisle. Besides, there *was* something familiar. . . .

Ten years earlier she had dated a boy named Kurt. He had been killed in a motorcycle accident several years after their relationship had ended.

Still she didn't answer. All her red lights were flashing; she just wanted this bum to leave her alone.

Coming closer, he repeated the question.

"Who *are* you?" she asked with an edge.

"Rick Chase."

She was surprised. Chase had been older than she when they attended high school, and she remembered him as a neat, fairly serious boy. In fact, he had dated her older sister briefly. There had been some talk, she recalled, about his getting into drugs later and taking a turn for the worse. She now believed it.

His blue jeans were grimy, as was the orange ski parka he wore. His hands and fingernails were badly stained, and he had a dirt smear on his face.

For a few moments the young woman and the stranger made small talk. She did her best to be polite, but she was uneasy. She wanted only to get away from him. Her former schoolmate even smelled bad.

After she broke off the conversation on the pretext of being busy she tried to stay out of his way. But her efforts were useless, as he seemed to look for ways to run into her again.

She finally suspended her shopping, though she was not through, and headed for the checkout stand.

He was waiting there.

"Where are you going in such a hurry?"

"To pay," she replied calmly.

"Listen, I need a ride."

"Sorry, I can't."

"I gotta get outta here right away."

On top of everything else, he seemed very paranoid —as spooked as a wild animal snared by civilization.

"Sorry." She waited in line, paid for her purchases, and headed for the exit.

He was right behind her in line, buying a single can of orange soda.

While he paid she hurried out the door.

"Wait!" he shouted.

She kept on until she reached her car.

By the time he caught up with her she had thrown her bags in the backseat and was seated behind the steering wheel, struggling to get her keys in the ignition. She had made sure the windows were rolled up and had locked the doors.

When he was about a foot away she got the key in and started the motor.

He reached for the door handle.

As she backed out of the parking space he was forced to let go. She drove away without another word. In the rearview she saw him turn back toward the market.

Relieved to be away, she could allow herself a bit of whimsy. Boy, she thought, that guy had *changed* since high school. She could hardly wait to call her sister.

In the first block of houses adjacent to Town and Country Village, Patricia Eastwick, of 2371 Tioga

Way, saw the bedraggled man wearing an orange jacket walking down her street around noontime.

She was fascinated by his progress because he made a point of veering to the porch of a house across the street and crossing in front of the living room window. The house was of particular interest to Eastwick because her brother-in-law lived there.

He was sitting in his living room at the time and noticed the stranger's approach.

When her brother-in-law came out of his house Eastwick waved to him.

"He walked right across my porch," her brother-in-law shouted, more in surprise than anger.

"I know," she replied, shaking her head.

The interloper was now heading down the street.

What was his story, Patricia Eastwick wondered, and just what in the world was he looking for?

A short distance down the street Richard Chase suddenly turned and headed toward the front door of 2360 Tioga Way—like its neighbors, a modest 1950s tract house.

Why he picked this house on this block none of us ever learned. There was a blue van parked in the driveway, signifying the definite possibility that someone was home. So clearly a daylight burglary was no longer his motive. No, Richard Chase was about to "progress" in his crimes.

Possibly he had noticed, through a window, the young woman alone in her home. Or—as we would later learn—Teresa Wallin, twenty-two, had gone to the Pantry Market an hour earlier to cash a ten-dollar check. Maybe he had spotted the brunette at the store or on her way home, after Nancy Holden had left him in the parking lot.

Chase slipped a .22-caliber semiautomatic handgun from a leather shoulder holster that was under his jacket as he moved up the porch.

When he reached the door he cocked the gun, ejecting a bullet. He coolly dropped it into the mailbox. Then, with his free hand, he reached for the doorknob.

The door was unlocked.

3

Blue-eyed Teresa Wallin had shoulder-length chestnut hair that she parted in the middle. Carrying a nicely proportioned 120 pounds on her five-foot, five-inch frame, this attractive woman's most remarkable feature, friends and loved ones concurred, was her smile. It epitomized, all agreed, her guileless charm and sweetness.

She loved her new home and took pride in keeping a neat house. Three bedrooms were really too many for her and her husband David, but they had plans.

As usual, things were tidy inside 2630 Tioga Way. One of the first things the lady of the house did each morning after washing the breakfast dishes was to make the king-size water bed in the master bedroom —no easy chore. But she attended to that, as she did most everything, with a carefree determination.

Teresa Wallin was crazy in love with her husband and with life. She was infectiously happy—right up to the moment that the front door of her house flew open, revealing an armed man in the doorway.

Those of us who later entered the house and saw her death's-head expression frozen in abject horror would agree that Teresa Wallin knew in those final seconds that she was about to die. She knew, and she fought it.

She had left the kitchen with a sack of garbage and was headed toward the front door. That was the easiest route to the garbage can. In another second or two she would have been at the door. Maybe, seeing the stranger on the porch, she could have slipped the lock in time. Or she could have run outside for help. But it was not to be.

She did not always lock the door when she was home alone during the day. It didn't seem a vital thing to do, since they lived in a nice neighborhood. But then—without warning—the intruder was in the open doorway.

She stopped in her tracks, dropping the garbage as Richard Chase slammed the door behind him.

When he raised the gun and aimed it at her she brought her hands up defensively. He capped two rounds. One entered the palm of her right hand, traversed up her forearm, and exited at her elbow. Continuing its spiraling but slowed ascent, the bullet nicked her neck. The other slug tore at full velocity through the topmost portion of her skull, entering on one side and exiting on the other.

She collapsed to the floor.

Chase rushed to her, knelt down, and held his smoking weapon less than six inches from her left temple.

He fired.

It was the coup de grace.

The killer reholstered his weapon and settled down to his task. He picked up her shoulders and dragged her to a bedroom. Dark bloodstains followed him down the hall. He left his victim for a moment and moved into the kitchen. He found what he wanted in a silverware drawer near the sink. He also picked up an empty yogurt cup from the spilled trash on the living room floor.

Then he returned to the bedroom.

He still had a lot of work to do.

David and Teresa Wallin had been married two and a half years, long enough to have settled into a fairly regular routine. Two evenings every week were set aside for bowling together. They had developed friendships with several other young married couples who had blended into an informal social group. Until Teresa took her new job with the state she had attended exercise classes with a girlfriend on Monday and Wednesday evenings.

David Wallin awoke at the crack of dawn on January 23, rose, and tiptoed around the house. It was Teresa's day off from her new job, and he knew she wanted to sleep late. He left the house at 7:45 and arrived at the linen company where he worked at five minutes to eight.

Employed as a delivery driver for a Sacramento linen company, on that morning he was to begin training a new driver. Together they were scheduled to make a run over the Sierra Nevada to Lake Tahoe.

It was a little before noon by the time they had the panel truck loaded. They drove toward Interstate 80 to start the haul over the mountains, but they didn't get far. They stalled in a service station at Auburn Boulevard and Fulton Avenue, just down the street from the Wallin house. A maintenance mechanic joined them, worked on the truck, told them everything would be all right, and left. But everything was not all right, and after the first steep grade up Interstate 80 the truck quit again. They were just outside the town of Newcastle at about the thousand-foot elevation. Luckily, a pay phone was nearby.

Once again Wallin called for help. The same maintenance man eventually showed up, bypassed the truck's electrical system, and got the engine started. The mechanic told Wallin the truck would not run very far, and he'd better head back for the barn. It was five o'clock by the time Wallin and his companion returned to the linen company, with their truck still fully loaded. They had traveled a little less than sixty miles round trip. It had been a bad day. They followed the company drivers' time-honored tradition and headed for Slick Willy's Bar at Fulton and Cottage avenues for a pitcher of beer. Then they each went home.

David Wallin parked his car in the driveway, next to the van. He got out and headed for the house, picking up the newspaper on the porch. The front door was unlocked. He opened it.

The house was dark, and that was not normal. He flipped on the light.

Shutting the door behind him, he noticed the bag of spilled garbage on the floor. That was strange, he thought. Very unlike Teresa.

Incongruously, the stereo was playing.

Brutus, the Wallin's full-grown German shepherd, was waiting just beyond the threshold, but Teresa was not.

That, too, was strange.

David shut the door behind him and called out for Teresa. As he did he flipped the light on and saw what he took for oil on the rug. There were more "oil" spots on the carpet, and a trail leading to the back of the house. Curious and concerned, he followed them down the shadowy hallway toward the master bedroom. The trail ended there.

The scene was cruel, horrible, unmerciful.

Later that day the complexions of veteran homicide investigators would turn ashen when they looked at the sight on the floor of the master bedroom.

It was then Wallin began screaming. The sound climbed across the scale, carrying a message of grief that rocked the neighborhood. People looked out their windows, and some even stepped outside.

There was no need for him to touch his dear Teresa. She was dead.

Her eyes were open. They were no longer the sparkling, loving windows that had, just that morning, opened the world to his wife's kind soul. Now they stared upward with a terror that was unimaginable.

4

I was in the middle of dinner with my family when Communications reached me at 6:54 that evening.

It had been a long day. I had been up since four o'clock that morning after responding, along with Detectives Habecker and Homen, to an officer-involved shooting. Homicide investigated all such incidents, whether or not a death resulted. (In this case, after a high-speed chase, the suspect in a van had tried to run over a deputy. The suspect was shot and wounded. It seemed clear to us that it was—in police jargon—a "righteous" shooting.)

Since Habecker and Homen had, I knew, just gotten home, too, after a tiring day, I decided to respond myself to the call for homicide detectives. (Our four-man bureau was working overtime as it was.)

I never did finish dinner that night, but before I could leave there were some important calls to make.

Informed that Patrol Sergeant Dean Johnson was

standing by at the Tioga Way crime scene, I contacted him through the dispatcher. I wanted to be sure the responding patrol units had secured the immediate area so that bystanders and others would be kept away. Sgt. Johnson assured me they had done so. Also, I verified that the Crime Scene Investigations (CSI) unit had been called.

In my next call I requested assistance from Metro Detail, which had a large pool of detectives on call that could be lent out to hard-pressed bureaus. We qualified. From the sound of it, I'd need all the help I could get.

I then dialed the coroner's office and notified them that we had another homicide in the East Area, and that they would be called later that night when we had finished our work at the scene. (No bodies were ever removed from a murder before detectives and CSI personnel completed their exhaustive investigation at the scene.)

Then I kissed my wife and drove off in my unmarked county car. Because all the pieces were in place, I didn't use my siren and red light like you see in the movies. The victim, I knew, would be there waiting for me.

I parked a block away from 2630 Tioga Way, well away from the crime scene. I hoped the Metro detectives would do the same. I didn't want any more murder evidence uncovered by reporters, thanks just the same.

From the trunk of my vehicle I pulled out a notepad and tape recorder. I made sure it was loaded with a sixty-minute cassette and that I carried an extra one.

My gun I left where it always was: in the trunk in a hard-shell suitcase. I hated the thing, and for that I took a lot of ribbing. It was still in my patrol holster and belt, one of those thick rawhide getups that beat cops have a baton and handcuffs and ammo and a zillion jangling keys attached to. My stint in patrol had been the last time I wore my gun on a regular basis. Since I'd been a detective I had kept it sequestered in the car. Homicide detectives don't often nab killers with their guns, but rather by using their heads. I was always getting nasty notes from some departmental bureaucrat informing me that I was delinquent on my firing-range qualification requirement. As often as I could I tossed these irritants into the circular file and gave them no further thought. I had never fired my gun at a human being, and I intend to end my career with that stellar record.

As I approached the crime scene I saw that members of the press, both electronic and print, were arriving in platoon strength. I knew our spokesman would have called and alerted them. That is departmental policy. It's better to control the press than to have to react to them constantly. If we were the first to tell what happened, then the media would at least *start* their coverage with the facts. For the moment they would have no contact with me, only with the press information officer. At a crime scene, and in the opening volleys of a homicide investigation, I did not have public relations high on my list of priorities.

It was 7:45 P.M. when I ducked under the yellow "Police Only" ribbon that cordoned off the side of Tioga Way where the Wallin residence was located. I directed the nearest deputy to extend the perimeter to the front lawns on the opposite side of the street for the entire length of the block. "I don't want *any* vehicles driving or parking on this street," I said firmly. "That includes the press."

This was a vital moment in any homicide investigation. The victim and crime scene were waiting for us—or should be—just as the killer had left them. Here, the first pieces of the jigsaw puzzle that made up most murder cases could be found. It was up to us not to overlook them.

A pristine crime scene exists only once. It can and will be recreated through photographs, lab tests, reports, and, later, through expert testimony at trial. But we get only one chance to step into the scene ourselves, with all our senses on keen alert. And to begin to understand the hows and whys of what the victim went through, and—most important—who committed the most inhuman crime of all.

In front of the Wallin house one of the deputies had the job of keeping a log of everyone who entered and left the house. No one—not even detectives or the coroner or the sheriff himself—would enter the premises without being logged. At least in theory, that was standard operating procedure for a crime scene.

Another deputy came up and informed me that the victim's parents had arrived.

I would talk to them myself. The victim's husband, I understood, was at a neighbor's house, giving a statement to a deputy.

I went to the parents. I told Leona and John Lahann how very sorry I was about their daughter. There was really nothing they could do here at the scene, I explained, and I suggested it would be better if they went home. I would send a detective to their house to talk to them and keep them updated on the investigation.

With that the Lahanns drove away. Teresa's mother was crying and on the verge of hysteria.

Eventually I began a slow-beat walk up to the Wallin house with CSI's Frank Davidson at my side. We were already looking for precious clues, studying the sidewalk, driveway, and front porch. As usual, we didn't know exactly what we were looking for, but we hoped there would be something, *anything,* left behind by the killer. A smashed cigarette butt. Matches. Something that would indicate his entry and/or departure path. In the mailbox we found his first calling card.

I left the cartridge where it was for now, but I noticed that it was .22-caliber. Though I wouldn't be sure until ballistics reported back days later, I had more than an inkling that our "East Area Killer" had struck again. And if so, he had gone from a random drive-by killing to something even more hideous.

I noticed there were no pry marks on the door or surrounding frame, meaning either the door had been unlocked or the victim had opened it. I flipped on my recorder and duly noted my observation.

At 8 P.M. exactly, according to the entry log, I walked into David and Teresa Wallin's home. No one had entered the premises since the responding patrol unit.

I stepped past the garbage. The bag had broken, and its contents were scattered across the living room.

I went to the spot where Teresa Wallin had been shot, where her blood had soaked into her own carpet.

My recorder was back on: "Two small brass shell casings on the living room floor," I intoned. "Leaving them in place, but they look like .22-caliber."

The FM stereo radio was still on; the musical background seemed surreal. We left it on, of course. Had the victim or the killer turned the radio on? Perhaps we could lift a print or two from the on-off switch and find out.

At that point we were interrupted. I was told that detectives from Metro were outside. Wayne Irey and two others.

I went outside for a few minutes and briefed the detectives on what needed to be done. They went off to start canvasing the area to learn what the neighbors had seen and heard, and I returned to the crime scene.

The large blood spot in the living room with its smaller satellites led us toward the bedroom and Teresa Wallin's corpse. Some of the spots merged, blended, and became drag marks. All led to the master bedroom.

"We are following trail of blood down hallway. . . ."

There was more blood on the floor of the bathroom, which was located off the hall that led to the master bedroom. Out of the corner of my eye I noticed what looked like blood in the wash basin. Had the killer washed his hands afterwards? "Check sink for blood."

Teresa was lying just inside the door to the master bedroom, her legs and feet pointing into the hallway.

If a cop is going to investigate homicides, he must get used to murder scenes. The body becomes just another piece of evidence—in fact, the most important evidence. There is no room for compassion. That is the theory. In truth, a cop could live a dozen lifetimes and not get used to pitiful sights like the body of Teresa Wallin.

She was flat on her back. Her turtleneck sweater had been pulled up, exposing her breasts. Her left nipple had been carved off, apparently by a knife. The same weapon, undoubtedly, had been used to cut open her torso, from just beneath her sternum to near her left hipbone. Not only were her innards visible, but a sizable portion of her intestine extended outside her body cavity.

Her blue corduroy pants and lime-colored panties were bunched at her ankles, and her knees were splayed open as if she'd been sexually assaulted. I did not assume the latter, naturally. That would be determined by lab tests. Some sexually deviant killers, I knew, pulled down clothing and elaborately positioned bodies so that their victims would be found in such humiliating poses.

What I felt at that moment about the victim was personal. This was *my* victim, and I was already starting to make that connection that every good homicide detective makes to each and every victim. It is both a professional bond and a personal one, and it continues throughout the course of the investigation. Professionally, you want to do the investigation as flawlessly as possible. Personally, you "own" the case, and you know you'll never put it out of your head until you solve it.

I would try to know almost everything about the victim. Importantly, through her corpse, I would also start to get to know the person who had done this to her. Indeed, he had left lots of clues, disgusting as they were, right with her. In what he did to her and how he did it he had revealed details of his warped thoughts and desires. In the end they might well be his undoing.

As I stayed next to her, remaining quiet, revolt and compassion welled up inside me simultaneously.

Then, in the time it might have taken me to snap my fingers, my detective's instincts began taking over. The body was evidence, the most important link to the person responsible. Through the matted blood in her hair and on her face I saw one clean bullet wound in her left temple. She would have died quickly from that shot, I knew. If it had been fired into her head in the living room, before the killer's other atrocities against her, then there was a merciful God after all. The look in her eyes revealed that she had died in fear and pain, but I prayed that the end had come quickly for her.

I noticed a lead pencil on the floor beside the body, and near it a book of matches. Beside them was a crumpled yogurt container covered with blood both inside and out. On the hardwood floor next to the container were several bloody ringlet-shaped stains. I had never seen anything like them and couldn't imagine what the ringlets were.

I left the house to the CSI technicians, who would examine and photograph the scene and collect further evidence. (Later that night they found several fresh shoe prints that left a diagonal design on the kitchen floor. Just in case, we checked the shoes of everyone who had entered the house. None matched the shoe prints in the kitchen.)

I exited the house at 8:30. There was a lot still to do, and I would stay at the crime scene coordinating those activities until after 2 A.M. When I left, the CSI team had not even worked its way to the kitchen. Their work was just that laborious.

When I came outside after viewing the body I immediately called Communications to confirm that a county pathologist and criminologist had been sent to the scene.

Next a cadre of officers was assembled and assigned to check restrooms and trash bins in the Town and Country shopping center for bloody items.

I assigned a Metro detective to interview David Wallin. He reported back shortly that the husband had been working during the time of the murder. Of course. The handiwork inside the house did not look like the result of a domestic quarrel.

An hour and a half passed before the detectives reported back after questioning everyone they could find in the Wallin block.

Three reports from witnesses were remarkably similar. Each mentioned seeing a "weird man" in the area. The neighbor who had seen the man walk brazenly across his front porch had been interviewed. So had another resident who saw a man walk across the front lawn of the house located right next to the Wallin property.

The descriptions of the "weird man" were similar. He was a white male in his mid-twenties, weighing about 150 pounds. And he was wearing an orange ski parka.

January 24, 1978

We didn't leave any gaps. A detective was told to find and question the newsboy when we learned from David Wallin that the *Sacramento Bee* had been delivered, as usual, and was on the porch when he arrived home.

By morning Detective Don Habecker had joined the investigation. He checked out the backyard of the Wallin residence. There he found Brutus, the Wallin's German shepherd, apparently completely intimidated by the happenings of the last twenty-four hours. He did not bark when Habecker approached him, but cowered. Family members told Habecker this was not the dog's normal behavior. The fact that Brutus had been inside the house when David Wallin had arrived home led family members to believe fervently that the killer must have been someone known by the family. I wasn't so sure. It had been my experience that watchdogs often didn't deliver as promised, and when needed were just as likely to run or hide as bark or bite.

While examining the backyard Habecker noticed that part of the lawn near the rear fence was under water. Some boards had been placed in the water and offered dry passage to the fence. The walkway had been used often. On the other side of the fence was a part of the parking area for the Town and Country shopping center. A gate opened where the boards reached the fence. Impressions of a diagonal pattern, seeming to match identically those of the kitchen-floor shoe prints, were visible on the damp boards.

But the trail was so indistinct Habecker decided it would be impossible for any type of photograph to record them. He was at last fairly sure, though, that the killer had left the Wallin property through the shopping center lot.

Fifteen minutes later Habecker was told by a woman who identified herself as the resident of a nearby house that her five-year-old daughter had seen a knife in the storm drain near her home. She led the detective and other deputies to a storm drain at the intersection of Shasta Way and Tioga Way. They found a knife lying about a foot below the grate.

A tire iron was used to remove the grate. With that out of the way a CSI investigator photographed the six-inch steak knife in the drain. The serrated blade was similar, Habecker realized, to the set of steak knives stored in the Wallins' kitchen. It was packaged and taken to the crime laboratory. (Later it was determined that the recovered knife had not been used by the killer.)

Meanwhile, inside the residence, detectives examining the master bedroom found a .300 Savage rifle and a .308 Winchester equipped with telescope sights. Teresa's murderer had not touched them. Blood stained the water bed that was the central piece of furniture in the master bedroom. Fortunately, it had not been penetrated by a knife or bullets. Had that happened, there would have been a fair-sized flood on the floor, possibly washing away some of our physical evidence.

Whatever had motivated the killer, it was not greed. When Teresa was found she was wearing a heart-shaped locket that appeared to be gold. It was strung from her neck by a chain that also seemed to be gold. Her right hand was adorned by a pair of rings. A red stone, which could have been a ruby, was mounted in one of them. A gold wristwatch was on her left arm. She wore a white metal ring, probably either silver or white gold, on her left index finger. A yellow metal ring with what appeared to be a diamond mounted on it (her engagement ring?) decorated her left ring finger. Her killer had left them, and their considerable value, on her hand. Also, the change from a $10.00 check Teresa had cashed at the grocery store earlier that morning was still in her purse.

Burglary and robbery were ruled out.

Again, one look in the bedroom had told me that.

The morning after her death Teresa Wallin's body was autopsied by Dr. Joseph Masters, a county pathologist. I assigned Detective Fred Homen to attend the procedure.

Actually, a pathologist and a criminologist had begun to work on the body as soon as it was transported to the coroner's office in the wee hours of the morning. An early X-ray revealed two projectiles lodged in Teresa's skull. They appeared to be copperjacketed .22-caliber bullets.

(After the bullets were recovered from the body, tests determined that they were fired from a .22 "similar" to the one that had killed Ambrose Griffin and had shot at the very lucky lady. That was as close to a match as we could get that time. Even science is not perfect.)

When Homen arrived at the coroner's office and learned of the second bullet in her head, he called me right away. He had heard two casings had been found early on at the house. But the defensive wound in the arm plus two in the head totaled three. "Looks like there's a third one, Ray," he reported.

After only four hours of sleep I was back at my desk, already on my sixth cup of black coffee.

"I know, Fred," I said wearily, slipping a pinch of long-cut Skoal inside my cheek. (I'd given up smoking years earlier. Some tradeoff, huh?)

Though I had not known until Homen's call where —or even if—a third bullet had actually struck our victim, I did know there had been a third shot fired inside the house. A couple hours before I'd left the scene a CSI investigator had come outside to tell me a third casing had been found on the living room floor in front of the couch. The same investigator had revealed that they were recovering latent prints in the house that had a distinctive zigzag pattern. They were very similar, he thought, to those found on latex rubber gloves.

Before the physicians went to work that morning, criminalist Alan Gilmore scanned the body with an ultraviolet light looking for evidence of rape. The ultraviolet rays would illuminate any external semen traces. (Today a laser is used for the same purpose.) Nothing was found. Other tests also failed to find any evidence of rape.

After the pathologist confirmed the tape recorder was running, the real medical work began.

Homen, standing to one side but not afraid to look at the details of the evidence being gathered before him, was taking his own notes. The "defensive-type wounds" in her palm and forearm were examined, he wrote, as were two "entrance-type gunshot wounds" in her head.

Dr. Masters then turned his attention to the killer's savage butchery. The abdominal wound "produced incising that indicated a profound depth of a minimum of six inches." So forceful had the killer's thrust with the knife been that the murdered woman's sternum and breast plate had been actually split open. Dr. Masters observed that the wounds that ripped open the sternum and chest cavity were the result of upward thrusts.

The abdominal wound, when expanded to view the inner damage, produced at least eight points where the instrument used by the assailant came to rest at the base and next to the spinal column.

"The kidneys were remarkable," Homen wrote in his report following the autopsy, "in that they were severed [by the assailant] and were both resting on the left side beneath the liver."

Homen, after observing and listening to Dr. Masters at work, came to this conclusion: "Based on the type and number of wounds coupled with the evidence of inner organs being tampered with, it is apparent that the assailant had explored the innards of the deceased."

The macabre findings had reached bedrock, I thought at this point as I read Homen's report later that day.

But I was wrong.

As noted by Homen in conclusion, Dr. Masters had removed Teresa Wallin's womb. Inside the pathologist found evidence of a three-month-old fetus.

5

Watt Avenue is a long street. Fifteen miles, to be exact. And it is a strange street. Tawdry, rundown, and congested in places, yet with intersecting avenues that form the boundaries of some of the most pleasant yet affordable upper-middle-class neighborhoods in the California state capital.

These suburbs seem to have grown by accident more than design. A great many homes were constructed during the early fifties following the war and were purchased with some of the state's first low-interest veterans' mortgage loans. These neighborhoods have aged just enough to have developed an arboreal maturity that makes them almost bucolic. Yet they have a solid, salt-of-the-earth personality. Real people live here—folks who drive off to work early in the morning and come home at night before the six o'clock news. Family-raisers nearly all, they are happy to own their own homes, complete with patio barbecues, fenced yards, and sometimes even a pool with a slide.

Along the fringes of these neighborhoods are several large shopping centers. They are convenient for the residents, but in places these centers provide an uneasy neutral zone between the haves and the have-nots.

Then there is the American River—and just how many city dwellers can boast that they have a real river in their front or back yard? It gathers all of its tributaries as it travels westward through the East Area, preparing for its confluence with the south-bound Sacramento River close to downtown. A net-work of narrow streams meanders through the neighborhoods before reaching the heart of the city. The banks are often lined with trees and bushes, and in countless places they provide shelter or hiding for just about anyone from young lovers to hoboes.

Murders are not unusual along some of these lonely, tree-studded stretches. One wino will kill another for his money or his bottle. There are occasional victims of rape and homicide left along the stream banks. Sometimes the body of someone who died or was killed in another place is hauled to one of the stream beds and dumped.

The area off Watt Avenue where Ambrose and Carol Griffin lived could be labeled one of the better resi-dential areas on that side of the city, adding to the shock of the drive-by shooting. Neighboring Del Paso Country Club, one of the county's finest and oldest golf and country clubs, is located off Watt Avenue only a few blocks away. None of us in the Homicide Bureau could afford membership there.

But things had "progressed" since the Griffin slaying. It was more than just a neighborhood aberration. We now knew we were dealing with a homicidal maniac, not your run-of-the-mill killer. He would strike and kill again and again until we caught him. A man who did the things he did to Teresa Wallin does not stop one day, get a job, settle down, and pay his parking tickets on time.

The reporters had heard and seen enough on Tioga Way that evening to whet their interest. It was a big story. They asked questions that were answered as honestly and accurately as possible. While striving to be sensitive to the dignity of the victim and family, I do not believe in misleading the press or the public.

The crime bulletin we distributed to other law enforcement agencies after the Wallin murder read as follows:

On January 23, 1978, between 0930 and 1330 hours, Teresa Lynn Wallin, twenty-two years old, was murdered in her residence at 2630 Tioga Way. She was shot three times with a .22-caliber weapon. The body was then mutilated by an incise wound in the abdomen. The weapon used was probably a sharp knife with a blade six inches or longer. Garbage was strewn over the living room floor. There does not appear to have been anything taken from the residence, and there is no evidence of forced entry.

The subject in the [attached] artist's sketch is wanted for a burglary that occurred on the same day at 2929 Burnece Street, approximately 1100 hours. The suspect defecated in the residence and urinated on clothes in the dresser drawers. The suspect was apparently preparing to remove a decorator sword and dagger but was surprised by the homeowners. The suspect was chased several blocks toward the direction of Watt and Marconi avenues.

The suspect description that went out with the bulletin was: white male adult, early to mid-twenties, 5' 10" to 6' 0", slim build, dark brown hair, blue Levi's, black tennis shoes, orange jacket.

I concluded with "This subject is wanted for questioning *only* in connection with this homicide," then signed off with my name and office phone number.

Never in the history of the Sacramento County Sheriff's Department had anyone reported a scene like that on Tioga Way.

Reflecting back now as I tell this story, I must confess that the bloody ringlets on the carpet next to Teresa Wallin's body went right over my head. I could see they were transfer patterns from something round —probably the yogurt cup. And the crime lab soon reported that the ringlet stains were human blood type A—the victim's type. Still, what this represented escaped me.

I was not ready to face the fact that we were dealing with a man who was to go down in homicide annals as the "Dracula Killer."

Since the new year we had investigated eight mysterious deaths in one twenty-nine-day stretch, and more than a few of the cases remained unsolved for some time to come:

- Dec. 29—Ambrose Griffin murder.
- Jan. 5—A forty-three-year-old man, the third party in a love triangle, was found shot to death in his bedroom. (Result: The suspect subsequently committed suicide in Richmond, California.)
- Jan. 8—A baby girl died at the hands of her abusive father. (Result: The father was convicted and served three years in prison.)
- Jan. 9—A man who barricaded himself in his apartment fired on responding deputies, who returned fire with several shotgun blasts that killed the suspect. (Result: justifiable homicide.)
- Jan. 17—A man was shot and killed in the parking lot of an apartment house. What began as a real mystery—"No suspects or vehicles seen leaving the area"—became a sensational murder case. (Result: Five years later several of the victim's relatives were convicted and sent to prison for planning and executing his murder.)
- Jan. 19—A baby boy was taken to a local hospital, where he later died of head injuries. (Result: The infant's mother was convicted and served three years in prison.)
- Jan. 23—Teresa Wallin's murder.
- Jan. 26—A convenience store clerk was found dead in the cold locker, shot in the head. (Result: the case remains unsolved to date.)

Like I said, we'd been kind of busy.

A crime wave of another type was also sweeping the east side of Sacramento: the "East Area Rapist" was still on the prowl. At the time he was in his second year of terrorizing the city, and a county-wide task force was operating to try to find and apprehend him. (The fact that Homicide, as well as other Sheriff's Department bureaus, had contributed detectives to this task force was why we were so shorthanded when our murder wave began.)

On December 2, 1977 the East Area Rapist had committed his twenty-eighth rape.

As well as we could we reconstructed Teresa's last day up to the time of her death. She had visited the Town and Country center next door between 9:30 and 10:30 on the morning of the twenty-third. We learned that from the clerk who had cashed her check that morning. We even took her check with us. The helpful clerk said she knew Teresa well because she shopped at the market often. The clerk remembered Teresa being one of few customers in the store at the time she cashed her check.

In the days that followed we interviewed scores of witnesses, some of which we had smoked out because they were friends, acquaintances, or fellow employees of one of the Wallins.

Among these were David Wallin's two sisters, who were interviewed in the living room of their parents' home. Actually, they had called us to say they had some new information. In the interview they told us in no uncertain terms that they believed one of

David's old flames might have been his wife's murderer.

They said the woman, whom I'll call Joyce Summers, was "very unhappy" when David had married Teresa.

When Teresa and David were married Summers had put a real damper on the wedding reception by following David around the room telling him how much she loved him.

Joyce Summers had also confided to one of David's sisters that she had once been into a "devil cult," and she claimed psychic powers and the ability to see into the future.

We had to think about that story. With a streak of male chauvinism I found irritating, I had just about let the violence of Teresa Wallin's murder eliminate from my mind the possibility that a woman might be the killer. But I did remember from my high school days Lady Macbeth and a woman scorned. How did it go? "Hell hath no fury . . ."

Considering the knife thrust that had actually cut through Teresa's sternum, however, and the strength needed to inflict that kind of damage, I still had serious doubts about a female suspect. On the other hand, David Wallin's ex-girlfriend did become someone we were interested in, and we set out to investigate her activities on January 23.

It didn't take us long to find out that while a very jealous and embittered Joyce Summers seemed to have some motive for the killing, her activities during the time the killing took place could be accounted for.

She was not our man.

6

Reports piled in, one atop the other. As always with a homicide investigation of this magnitude, the challenge was separating the wheat from the chaff.

Sightings of a "strange" man were reported in the days that followed the Wallin murder. It seemed clear that someone who fit our suspect's description was still stalking the East Area. Only he appeared to be on the move, out of Teresa Wallin's Town and Country neighborhood and into an adjacent residential area that encircled Country Club Centre shopping area.

Numerous reports came from that area.

A woman who lived on Park Estates Drive reported hearing a noise and a knock at her door at about 12:30 on the afternoon of January 24 (the day after the Wallin murder). She found a man on her threshold who was unshaven and dirty. He asked if the woman had any old magazines and seemed upset when she said she had none. When he asked a second time, she closed the door.

Then there was a couple who lived on nearby Sunview Drive. At about eleven o'clock that same morning a man walking along the street caught their attention when he stopped in front of a neighbor's home and looked around. He apparently saw the "dog on duty" sign and moved on. The woman asked her husband to keep an eye on the man, and he did. When the stranger reached the couple's home he knocked on the door and asked for magazines. Told there were none available, he left. Later the woman saw him pass again, a few magazines under his arm. The man was slender with long messy hair. He wore an orange jacket.

That same day a woman alone in her home on Brentwood Road heard her doorbell ring. She found a disheveled and dirty man at the door asking for magazines. He specifically mentioned *Mad* and *Cosmopolitan.* When she told him she didn't have those particular publications he said he would take any she did have. She told him it would take a while to gather them, but she would leave her surplus magazines on the porch. When he said he didn't think he would remember the address she offered to write it for him. He promised to return in a few days.

The next day a man appeared at a home on Pennland Drive. He asked for magazines, and when told none were available, he departed. Described by the homeowner as thin, long-haired, and needing a shave, he then walked from door to door along the street.

(On January 25th, a pair of deputies interviewed a couple who had sold two Lab puppies to a "skinny, stringy-haired man" who drove a "ratty" Ford Ranchero. They had thought it strange at the time that the man didn't appear to care about the sex of the puppies or even much about their appearance. The next day, the couple found one of the other puppies from the litter dead on their rear patio. The pup had been shot, and its stomach had been split wide open. In their interview, the couple had been asked if anyone "suspicious" had been around the dogs recently, and they immediately remembered the strange puppy buyer. The deputies alerted me to their report, and I ordered the dog's body to be autopsied, a first for me. A veterinarian, and eventually Dr. Pierce Rooney, one of Sacramento's best known pathologists, were able to recover only fragments of bullets from Lab's body. They were, however, able to identify the projectile as a .22 caliber. They also determined that the animal had been tortured, eviscerated and some of its internal organs removed.)

At noon on January 26 a woman was sitting near the open front door of her home on Meadowbrook Road. Suddenly she realized a man was standing there. He was dirty, his dark brown hair was stringy, and he was very thin. He looked at her briefly, then moved on.

Twice more on that day the same man was seen. Once he appeared at a home on Merrywood Drive. He did not identify himself after ringing the doorbell. The young woman who lived there asked what he wanted, and he said, "Magazines." She asked what he wanted with magazines, and he said he intended to read them. She refused to give him any magazines, and the man left. He was, she said, thin, pale, and dirty. He was wearing a dirty orange coat. The woman said she "got a very bad feeling about him." He stared at her door for a frightening moment after she closed it, then moved on to the next house.

We expanded our canvas of the Wallin neighborhood to include everyone living in area whether or not they'd been home on January 23.

If, however, it turned out that Teresa Wallin had known her murderer—as her family steadfastly believed—the field of suspects would eventually narrow. We did continue along these lines, talking to her friends, relatives, co-workers, and former employers. While not tainting these efforts with any bias, I had little doubt that Wallin had been killed by someone she did *not* know. And that that same someone had killed Ambrose Griffin and shot at the woman in her kitchen.

Several times a day I studied the sketch of our suspect. We had flooded the town with this likeness. But how accurate was it? Sightings of a man who looked like him kept coming in, but always after the fact. Not one patrol unit—and patrols in the area had been beefed up—had yet stopped this man for questioning. We always knew where he *had* been, never where he was.

I didn't like that dirty, skinny guy in the orange jacket who went door to door being a step ahead of us.

Friday, January 27, 1978

Evelyn Miroth, thirty-eight, a single mother, lived at 3207 Merrywood Drive, in the heart of the Country Club Centre neighborhood, with her two sons, Vernon, thirteen, and Jason, six.

The still-attractive divorcée had not resigned herself to the role of a spinster. She had a regular boyfriend named Bill, who was fifty-one. Though she did not work other than baby-sitting a relative's child when needed, she was active, had lots of friends and relatives in the area, and was a busy hostess on most weekends.

One of her closest friends lived directly across the street. Neone Grangaard, who worked the graveyard shift at the Sacramento Post Office, also had two children, one of whom was Jason's age, six.

The weather had changed radically toward the end of January both in the Sierra Nevada and on the valley floor. A cold front moving in from the Pacific brought snow into the lower levels of the mountains and an early-morning chill across the valley floor.

Neone Grangaard, deciding to take advantage of the snowfall and her having the day off, planned to make a day trip into the nearby Sierra Nevada to let the children play in the snow. She called Evelyn that morning to see if she wanted to come along.

Evelyn said she was sorry to miss it, but she was baby-sitting her sister-in-law's twenty-month-old boy. "But can Jason go with you?" she asked hopefully. "He'd love it."

Neone was delighted to include Jason.

At 9:05 A.M. Evelyn called her friend and asked if she could plan on leaving a little later than their scheduled 10 A.M. starting time. Evelyn explained that she wanted to go to a nearby sporting goods store and rent a pair of snowshoes for her son.

Shortly thereafter Neone looked out her front window and saw the red station wagon that belonged to Evelyn's friend, Danny Meredith, parked in Evelyn's driveway. As she was watching she saw Meredith come out, get in the car, and leave. She wondered if Evelyn had signed him up to go rent the snowshoes.

Neone didn't look for or notice any other activity at her friend's house in the next hour and a half. But at 10:30 she looked out her window and saw that the station wagon was back, again parked in Evelyn's driveway. It was facing the garage door, which had been open all morning. Earlier in the morning, around 8:30, Evelyn had mowed her front lawn and then left the garage open.

A half hour passed with still no word from Evelyn. Anxious now to get started on the snow trip and irritated that Evelyn hadn't sent Jason over by then, Neone sent her six-year-old daughter Tracy across the street to see what was keeping Jason.

Tracy went to the Miroths' front door and knocked. She looked in the front window and saw no one and nothing unusual. But the little girl would remember, later, having seen some kind of movement inside the front room. No one answered the door, so Tracy returned to her home. It was 11:10 A.M.

By 11:30 Neone was getting anxious. Prepared to leave with or without Evelyn's boy, she took her daughter by the hand and crossed the street. Neone noticed that the red station wagon was now gone.

She rang her friend's doorbell. No one replied.

Neone Grangaard didn't know whether to be angry or frightened. Evelyn Miroth was not the type of person who stood up a friend without a word.

She walked to the home of Catherine Belli, Evelyn's next-door neighbor, and asked if she had seen Evelyn leave with Jason and Danny. The neighbor said she hadn't but told Neone there was probably nothing to worry about.

Shortly after noon Neone had had enough. She decided she and her daughter would go to the snow without Evelyn's boy. They climbed into their car and pulled out of the driveway. Neone stopped when she saw another neighbor taking a petition door to door for signatures. She confirmed to Neone that there was no one home at Evelyn's.

"It seems so suspicious," Neone said, shaking her head. "It just isn't like Evelyn."

Just then Nancy Turner, another neighbor who was a good friend of Evelyn's, arrived from an all-morning shopping trip. Briefed on the suspicious events of the morning, Turner decided to take action. She went to the rear of the Miroth home, knocked on the back door, then tried the knob. The door was open.

Nancy Turner entered the house. She walked through a family room and the kitchen and then into the living room. She screamed, a short, staccato little scream, then she shouted loudly. With that she fled.

Outside she yelled: "Someone's here, all right, but something's awfully wrong. He's on the floor, and there's blood all over the place. Call for help!"

Nancy's grim discovery brought a swift reaction by the people on that block of Merrywood Drive. Across the street were two men driving a Salvation Army truck that had been dispatched to pick up an old sofa. They announced that the truck was equipped with a radio and said they would contact the Sheriff's Department through their switchboard.

Comments started flying right away about the driver of the red station wagon. Everyone on the block knew him, at least by sight. He was about fifty and had been spending a lot of time with Evelyn and the children. Once he'd taken them to Disneyland, and another time they had stayed at a Marriott Hotel for the weekend. He was a thin man, gray-haired, with sharp facial features. No one was really sure if Evelyn's boyfriend Bill knew or approved of him.

After making their call the Salvation Army workers, who were the only men on the scene, volunteered to go inside and see if they could help. But when they peered through the living room window and saw the man lying on the floor surrounded by dark stains they decided to sit tight.

Sheriff's Deputy Ivan Clark arrived at the scene at 12:43 P.M. Communications had assigned him a "welfare check, man down" call at 3207 Merrywood Drive. Sounded routine enough to Clark—probably just a drunk passed out on a lawn or in his house.

The fact that several people had gathered outside the residence didn't mean anything to the deputy; that happened on most neighborhood disturbance calls. A couple of the neighbors expressed their concern for the occupants of the house, something about a little boy who was supposed to go on a snow trip but never came out. And about someone else seeing a man on the living room floor.

Clark assured the neighbors he would have a look inside and report back to them. He still thought he was dealing with a drunk.

Clark entered the back door, walking cautiously, as he had been trained. He had no sooner crossed the threshold than he saw the man lying on the floor near the hall. What looked like blood had soaked into the rug beside the body.

The deputy knelt next to the body and couldn't help but notice gunshot wounds to the head.

When he looked up from the body he could see into the bathroom. He saw blood all over the bathroom floor and what looked like bloody water in the bathtub.

What in the hell? he thought.

His eyes wandered further down the hallway.

The door to the master bedroom was open.

A woman lying on the bed. She was nude, her legs splayed open. Her abdomen had been ripped from sternum to lower belly, and internal parts were hanging out.

Having seen a video of the Teresa Wallin murder scene in patrol briefing, the deputy made the immediate connection to what he now saw in the bedroom.

Clark rushed outside and called Dispatch, requesting a supervisor and asking that Homicide be notified. Apparently he was in a "dead zone" in terms of radio transmission, because Dispatch kept saying he was "garbled" and asking him to repeat. By the time they finally understood him he was yelling so loudly that he was sure they would be able to hear him downtown without a radio.

The next thing he did, also correct, was to seal the crime scene.

Ivan Clark, though, was one very shaken deputy.

7

We have a custom in Homicide that has evolved over the years. We make a point of finding time daily to talk informally without the interruptions that are inevitable in police work. For a constructive hour or so we are undisturbed. We brainstorm, toss leads back and forth, and pick apart one another's pet theories. Phone calls don't reach us easily, and the top brass isn't around to ask a lot of questions we have to answer.

How do we do it?

Simple. We have lunch together.

At 12:55 P.M. on January 27 we were walking through the main lobby, heading for lunch. Usually we slipped out the back way, but today, for some reason I no longer remember, we went out the front.

As we moved toward the double doors that would take us to the street I glanced nonchalantly toward the reception desk. The deputy on duty frantically flagged me over. In her other hand she cradled a phone receiver.

"Patrol unit reports a one eighty-seven," she said in effective shorthand for Penal Code Violation 187: homicide.

When she gave me the Merrywood Drive address my stomach did a back roll. The Country Club Centre area that our suspect had been casing for days!

I asked for more.

"Several people down," she said, shrugging. "That's all I got."

Communication had relayed the urgent call from Deputy Clark just seconds earlier. The front-desk deputy had been trying to track me down at the very moment I walked past.

I decided to take our entire Homicide Bureau to the crime scene. Having all of our detectives free at the same time was a rare occurrence. If the call turned into what I most feared, I would need every hand I could get.

We took several cars.

In the noontime traffic it took me twenty minutes to get to the east side. In that time I spoke by radio several times to the supervisor on the scene, a Patrol Sergeant. I also made sure the coroner had been notified and advised that we needed a pathologist and a criminalist.

The Patrol Sergeant seemed to have things under control. He assured me that the crime scene had been sealed and that nobody would be allowed inside before I got there. As always, I wanted to eliminate, or at least reduce, the chances of crime-scene contamination and lost evidence.

66

I asked the supervisor to set up a nearby command post, and at 1:19 he reported back that a church parking lot off of Merrywood and Highridge Drive had been commandeered. I directed him to send all responding units to the parking lot so the street wouldn't clog up.

Three minutes later I arrived at the Merrywood and Highridge intersection. Much to my displeasure, it was jammed solid with a combination of sheriff's vehicles, Highway Patrol units, and privately owned cars. A large crowd had gathered on the street, straining to see what had happened.

I saw immediately that the area sealed off with ribbons was woefully small. (I guess, now that I think of it, after our experience with the TV crew finding the casing on the street, expanding the perimeter is almost always the first thing I do at a crime scene.) I directed that the sealed-off area be expanded.

I chose Detective Sergeant Jim Bevins of the Metro Detail to lead the detail that would canvas the neighborhood for leads.

Now it was time to have a look inside.

I moved toward the property with Bruce Clemenson of CSI at my side.

Deputy Ivan Clark, a tough, timeworn officer, was still guarding the front door. No one had gotten past him, I was willing to bet. I noticed that his face was an unusual pasty gray. Clark was case-hardened. Whatever was inside had to be awful.

We went through the open garage. A gold Chevrolet with a white vinyl top was parked inside. The garage was dusty—good breeding ground for latent fingerprints.

The yard was fenced behind the garage, and a gate closed it off. It was shut but not latched. We walked through it to the rear patio and across it to the back door of the residence. It was also open and standing ajar. There were some bloodstains on the door near the latch on the inside. It was through that door our beat patrolmen thought the killer might have entered. The bloodstains told me he had probably left by the same route. A cigarette butt on the porch was duly collected by Clemenson.

I saw that the porch floor around the cigarette butt was sprinkled fairly heavily with grass clippings. I remembered a Toro lawnmower had been standing just inside the gate when we entered the backyard.

When we proceeded further into the kitchen we found part of the sink, which was separated into two sections, full of murky gray water. Most of the kitchen drawers had been opened and apparently searched. There was blood of some description on one drawer.

Nearby, on the tiled surface of the sink board, was a knife about six inches long.

We moved into the living room. A man was lying facedown on the floor. His body extended across the hallway. His face was buried in the carpet, his right arm extended above his head and the left hand pointed toward his feet. He was dressed in tan trousers, plaid shirt, green vest, and beige windbreaker. From the appearance of his windbreaker, which had been pulled aside, and the position of his ankles, which were crossed, it appeared that the dead man had been turned over by someone. I could see gunpowder tattooing on the side of his head. Above his left ear there appeared to be an entry wound. The gunpowder tattooing around the wound suggested he had been shot at extremely close range.

Two live .22-caliber shell cartridges were found on the living room carpet. A spent cartridge was lying nearby, and there were two holes, which appeared to have been made by bullets, in the wall near the kitchen door.

A telephone had been knocked off its stand in the corner of the living room. The thought passed through my mind that one of the victims might have tried in desperation to call for help.

An empty coffee cup was lying on the floor of the hallway near the bathroom door. The tub in the bathroom was full of water that was stained red. A pile of what appeared to be woman's clothing was lying on the floor next to the bathtub.

Walking in tandem with CSI Clemenson, I entered the master bedroom at the south end of the house.

Evelyn Miroth was lying on her back. A gaping wound had ripped open her abdominal cavity. It didn't take an expert to see how strikingly similar it was to the mutilation done to Teresa Wallin. Her position on the bed was such that she was on the verge of falling off the bed. A seashell necklace was all she was wearing.

A large butcher knife stained a cardinal red was on the floor next to the woman's left hand. Another carving knife was on the bed next to her head.

Her hair was wet, as if it had been recently washed but not dried. Remembering the clothes in the bathroom and the stained water in the tub, I wondered if she'd been taking a bath when surprised by her killer. Up to that point—having been prepared, after the

Wallin scene, for what I might find—I had been doing all right. Psychologists call the studied reaction of homicide detectives at the scenes of crime "isolation of effect." We remove ourselves emotionally from what we're looking at and what we're doing. Do it any other way and you'll not last long in this job.

The murders were terrible. But I could look at the dead man lying across the hallway from the living room, realize he had been taken down by a head shot, and remove myself from the scene emotionally.

The woman on the bed had been murdered about as savagely as possible. The head wound was obvious, delivered directly above her right eye, and there seemed little doubt it would have been fatal. But had it come first, as with Teresa Wallin, or last?

Still I was the aloof, impersonal detective, weighing the evidence, no matter how gruesome.

For a while the woman dominated the scene in the bedroom. Her wounds, her death, had been the work of a madman with a unique and ugly signature. Everything pointed to it being the same killer who had savagely attacked Wallin.

The savagery at the Wallin scene had been repeated down to the last detail. Not repeated, I corrected myself, but exaggerated. There were more bodies this time.

CSI Officer Clemenson was busy photographing everything. But then his attention was drawn to something on the other side of the bed that I could not see from where I was standing.

I moved toward the bed.

There was the limp, fully clothed body of a boy I

would later learn was Jason Miroth. The little fellow had been shot in the head.

Before the murderer changed the family's plan that morning, Jason had been all ready for his snow trip to the mountains. He was wearing new maroon trousers, a striped turtleneck sweater, and shiny brown oxfords.

All my carefully groomed instincts escaped me at the sight of the dead boy. I was simply overwhelmed by the murder of this preschooler who looked to be (and was) the same age as my youngest boy. That horrible thought kept reverberating in my mind: He's Gregory's age. Oh, my God.

For the next several minutes I was not a detached homicide detective at all, but a father grieving over the senseless murder of his own son.

Outside a continually swelling crowd had been attracted to Merrywood Drive. What was different about this scene was the fact that responding with the curiosity seekers were a growing number of off-duty deputies and other peace officers who, knowing that their city would be in a state of near-panic with new gruesome murders, came to help. We put them to work in a hurry.

For a while I tried to direct single-handedly two operations from the command post. The first was to get a well-organized team into the residence, one with sufficient experience to process the information available without contaminating the scene. We didn't want to disturb the dust or the atmosphere if it could be avoided. I soon decided to put Detective Homen in charge of the efforts inside the house so I could keep my attention on the outside canvasing operation and the development of possible leads from witnesses.

I wanted everyone who had been near Merrywood and the surrounding areas that day questioned. Moreover, I wanted to know if any strange characters had been seen in the area that day, and to have their descriptions.

I carry in the trunk of my car maps of every neighborhood in the county. We opened and spread out the maps of the East Area and carefully detailed the assignments of every canvasing officer.

The nearby Country Club shopping center was jammed with the cars of post-holiday shoppers. That did not make life any easier for any of the large squad of deputies detailed to record the license numbers of each and every car parked there. That sounds tough, and maybe it was. But if we got lucky, it could provide us a clue to the killer's identity.

CSI uncovered one solid clue early on at the house on Merrywood Drive. Someone, while the blood was fresh, had walked through wearing a pair of athletic shoes. The sole of the shoes left a distinctive diagonal pattern in the soil. The pattern the shoes left on the bloody floor of the residence was similar to diagonal sole prints we had found at the Wallin home. Again we checked the shoes of everyone known to have entered the crime scene to determine if the pattern was left behind by the killer or by some cop or witness present at the scene. We found nothing like it.

One of the canvasing officers found an eleven-year-old girl on the block who remembered seeing a man around the victim's residence at approximately 11 A.M. She described him as being in his early twenties

—making him much younger than Meredith, the only other man known to have been around the Miroth house that morning. The girl remembered that the suspect had on a loud-colored jacket but couldn't recall the color.

Before long we learned the identities of the people who had been killed. The woman, of course was Evelyn Miroth, and the boy her six-year-old son, Jason. The man in the living floor was her friend, Daniel Meredith. Apparently Meredith had left the house safely once after his first visit that morning. He had not been so lucky the second time around. It seems likely when he had reentered the residence when the killer was on his rampage.

I was advised about the missing red station wagon belonging to Meredith. I remembered thinking his body had been turned over; it now occurred to me that the killer might have been looking for Meredith's car keys. We immediately put out an all-points bulletin for the stolen vehicle, listing the make, year, and license number.

Still in that part of the investigation when things move lightning-quick, I was told by a Metro detective at 3:30 P.M. that a woman, Karen Ferreira, had just arrived at the scene and stated that she had left her twenty-two-month-old son David with Evelyn Miroth earlier that morning. The victim was baby-sitting the boy. Had we found his body?

The answer was no.

Exactly three minutes later Fred Homen emerged from the Miroth residence with news that CSI had found a bullet hole in the pillow in a crib located in one bedroom. I remembered passing, on my tour of the house, a bedroom that had an empty crib inside. But with the degree of mayhem in the rest of the house, the room had not yet gotten much attention from us. The hole, Homen explained, was right where a sleeping child's head would be. "There's blood, too," Homen said ominously. "Lots of it."

The likelihood that we had a fourth victim seemed inescapable. The crime-scene team searched in every possible hiding place but came up empty-handed. Just where was David Ferreira's body?

A half hour later the baby's father, Tony Ferreira, who was Evelyn's brother, arrived at the scene. The owner of a gymnasium and health food store in North Sacramento, he joined his wife, who was being interviewed at a nearby residence by Detective Carol Daly. Karen, a nurse employed at the Sacramento Medical Center, had told us she hurried to the scene after hearing via news radio about a multiple murder on Merrywood. Her worst fears were true.

The child's mother was able to give us a fair inventory of the items that had accompanied her infant son to the Miroth home. Using that as a checklist, Homen and the CSI team found the complement of infant-sized garments. These included a brown turtleneck sweater, a pair of brown trousers, and a blue sleeper, found lying on the floor next to a recliner in the living room. A plastic bag that contained wet clothing, including rinsed-out cloth diapers, was also found. Baby's high shoes were found in another diaper bag with clean diapers and white socks. An empty plastic baby bottle was on the floor next to the diaper bag, and near it a hooded blue infant's coat. Virtually everything belonging to little David was there—except the clothes he had been wearing when he was dropped off.

Did we have a kidnapping on our hands? That didn't seem probable due to the physical evidence found in and around the crib. Assuming the baby had only been wounded, why would the assailant have taken the child with him? And if the boy had been killed, as the bullet and blood suggested, why would the killer have taken the body? The latter was actually two questions. Why would he have taken the chance of leaving the scene of his crime with evidence of his deeds? And why would he have wanted the boy's body?

(I would later learn, of course, that the neighbors had rung the bell at the Miroth house after the red station wagon had returned and while it was still parked in the driveway. When I did, I wondered if these actions had caused the killer to hurry. Had he taken the boy with him because—he had not finished whatever he wanted to do to the body?)

CSI reported back with more details on the crib. The pillow and the top sheet were covered with what appeared to be human blood. A spent .22-caliber casing was lying on the bottom sheet. The bullet had pierced the pillow slip but not the pillow, and the bullet was found lying atop the pillow just under the slip. A blood trail led away from the room.

That afternoon we had to leave the devastated Ferreiras with this simple truth: We did not know where their infant son was, but in all likelihood he, too, had fallen victim. We assured them we would have every available officer searching for him—or his body.

County Pathologist Dr. Pierce Rooney, examining the bodies at the scene, told us he believed the deep slashes across Evelyn Miroth's abdomen were post mortem. He pointed out that despite the massive cuts there had been little bleeding. (Because the heart is no longer pumping blood, dead people don't bleed excessively.)

Dr. Rooney then detailed something I had not noticed in the bedroom. In his careful physician's like manner he said, "There is a series of rings in the carpet next to her body." Not stopping, he speculated that they could have been made by human blood that was contained in a pail or pan next to the bed.

The mysterious ringlets . . . first found beside the body of Teresa Wallin, and now next to Evelyn Miroth.

I felt a chill that had nothing to do with the weather.

8

5 P.M., January 27, 1978

A sizable contingent of deputies had been assigned to
cruise through lots, both public and private, and
record the license numbers of every car parked in the
greater Country Club Centre area. I had ordered this
sweep on the chance that the killer might have parked
his car in the area and not yet returned to pick it up.
Also, of course, they were directed to search for
Daniel Meredith's missing station wagon.

It was Detective Sergeant John Irwin who found
Meredith's red vehicle parked in the lot of the Sandpiper Apartments at 3535 Marconi Avenue, exactly
1.3 miles from the Miroth residence. Like I said, most
breaks in this line of work are the result of good solid
police work.

I was told that when Irwin first radioed in his
discovery and requested a tow truck he had sounded
like a man who had won the lottery for us. In a way, he
had.

Finding the vehicle had accomplished one major goal. It helped us pinpoint the killer's activities to an area inside what we would soon identify as his area of operations.

Detectives responded to the Sandpiper Apartments and obtained from the building manager a list of the people to whom the parking stalls were assigned. We checked out every one of the residents, which took the rest of that day. It netted no suspects, but we felt we were closer to our killer than we had ever been.

At the time we didn't realize just how close.

A wooden fence was all that separated the Sandpiper Apartments from another large apartment complex situated just around the corner. Apartment 15 of the Watt Avenue complex was, at most, one hundred yards away from where Meredith's station wagon had been abandoned.

Richard Chase had all but taken the stolen vehicle home with him. It made sense for him to park so close, considering what his cargo had been that day and what he undoubtedly carried under his arm into his apartment.

The body of little David Ferreira.

Our latest crime bulletin went out that afternoon to all news outlets:

Miroth Homicide
3207 Merrywood Drive

At approximately 1239 hours, Friday, January 27, 1978, a call was received by the Sheriff's Communication Center of an apparent homicide at 3207 Merrywood Drive, adjacent to Country

Club Centre. Found at the scene were three victims. A while male adult, identified as Daniel J. Meredith, age fifty-two, was found lying on the floor, partially in the living room and hall of the residence, apparently shot in the head. Meredith is a friend of the family who was evidently visiting when the murder occurred. Meredith is reportedly the godfather of one or more of the Miroth children.

Evelyn Elizabeth Miroth, age thirty-six, was found on the bed. She was found with a large cut down the middle of the abdominal area. She may also have been shot.

Found on the floor at the foot of the bed was Jason Miroth, age six, apparently shot in the head.

Several small-caliber shell casings were found scattered in different parts of the residence. Two kitchen knives were also found that were apparently used in the homicide.

A possible fourth victim is missing from the residence. He is David Michael Ferreira, age twenty-two months. Ferreira was left at the residence at 7 A.M. to be baby-sat by Mrs. Miroth. The child has not been found.

A 1972 Ford station wagon, fire-engine red, license number 917 KCO, was determined to be missing from the driveway of the residence. The vehicle was later located at 3535 Marconi Avenue in an apartment house complex.

Mrs. Miroth is divorced from Vernon F. Miroth, age thirty-four. They have two other children, Laurie, fourteen, who resides with her father, and Vernon, age twelve, who was away at school at the time the murders occurred.

It has been tentatively established that the killings occurred sometime between 10:30 A.M. and 12:30 P.M. The canvasing in the area turned up no witnesses who heard shots or saw anything suspicious. There are no suspects at this time.

It was true we had no suspects.

But Detective Mike Hash of the East Area Rapist task force, one of the officers who responded to the Sandpiper Apartments, produced us a suspect almost instantly.

No sooner had Hash arrived than he spotted a scruffy-looking white male in his mid-twenties standing about fifty feet away, watching the activity around the station wagon. Hash thought the man resembled the sketch we had released of the burglary suspect on Burnece Street.

When the man noticed the detective giving him the once-over, he turned and headed into the apartment complex.

Hash didn't let him get away.

The detective had the man identify himself by showing a driver's license. The man was wearing blue jeans, a corduroy shirt, and a green parka vest. He had collar-length hair that looked quite dirty. He claimed to be a laborer for a local equipment company.

"What's going on?" the man asked.

"We're investigating a stolen car," Hash answered.

"All of this for a *stolen* car? Is it because of those people being murdered and cut up?"

Hash knew we had released some details of the

killings, including the fact that the bodies had been mutilated. But still, the combination of the man's familiarity with the murders and likeness to the sketch had the detective bothered.

More questions ensued, and when Hash remained unconvinced he asked the man to accompany him downtown to the Sheriff's Department for further questioning.

The man agreed.

Keith Roberts, twenty-three, was brought downtown and thoroughly questioned. He was photographed and fingerprinted. He cooperated fully. He was even shown the artist's sketch of our burglary suspect, and he noted the similarities without any hostility or signs of apprehension. He agreed to sign consent forms that allowed us to search his blue knapsack and his living quarters.

It was shortly after eight o'clock in the evening when the man was taken by our deputies to one of the interview rooms on the third floor in the Detective Division at Sheriff's Department headquarters. There he told Hash he had spent the night and early morning of the twenty-seventh at his brother's house in the East Area. Until his brother was married recently, he said, he had lived with him there. Presently he was spending most nights on a couch at his mother's apartment. Sometimes, he said, he stayed at his girlfriend's apartment near the Del Paso Country Club.

Later on the morning of the twenty-seventh he went to the bank, he said, joined his girlfriend on a shopping expedition, then returned with her to his mother's place.

Told by his mother that someone must have called the sheriff because the parking lot was filled with squad cars, he went out to see what was happening. That was what he was doing when the detective came up to him.

He said he had read of the Wallin killing. When shown a newspaper photograph of the young woman he recognized her as a former classmate at Encina High School. He knew her maiden name immediately.

Two items of interest were found when the knapsack and his living quarters were searched. An orange nylon windbreaker was found hanging in his closet among his other clothes, and a pair of Adidas sport shoes caught our attention briefly until we examined their soles and discovered they were pebble-grained.

In the end he was driven back home. His being brought in had been strictly routine, and once we checked his alibi we harbored no further suspicions about him.

Later that night another would-be suspect from the same neighborhood was brought downtown to be questioned after he'd become agitated and violent with canvasing officers. Though he would tell us very little, because of his extreme behavior we ended up dropping him off at Sacramento Medical Center for mental observation.

Descriptions of other possible suspects flooded in. A detective spotted a suspicious character in a Watt Avenue coffee shop and investigated. The man was occupying a booth all by himself. He was scruffy and dirty—not at all the type to be carrying a jeweled dagger. The man said the jeweled weapon belonged to his father, and he had simply shown it to the woman sitting next to him. He had been curious, he said, about its value.

The detective looked the man over. He was about five feet nine inches tall, had brown, shoulder-length hair, and was blue-eyed. The dagger he carried was eighteen inches long, made from brass, and similar to ceremonial weapons carried by members of a local temple of the Masonic Order of Shriners. A check with the Records Section revealed the man had been arrested for a variety of crimes, including burglary, but he was not currently on probation or parole or wanted for any crime. Neither had he been concealing the ornate dagger. He was not detained when the questioning was completed. The detective turned him loose reluctantly, but we had no grounds for holding the man.

Several other "suspects" were brought in that night and the next morning. It was all part of the case work. We had not forgotten about David Ferreira either. I had assigned a squad of detectives to search for the baby or to find his remains. So far their efforts were netting zero.

More often than not, suspects who are eventually charged with murder are questioned repeatedly before evidence is developed against them and they are actually arrested. Sometimes the process can go on for months. Immediate arrests in homicides are generally made only in "smoking gun"–type killings, where no questions exist as to the identity of the shooter. And contrary to what is often seen on television, it is the rare murder suspect who leaves town. Usually they are individuals who have no resources or other places to go.

It's always a morbid fear of ours that we have brought in the right man but let him go for the wrong reason. We are always second-guessing ourselves with great amounts of anguish. Did we ask him all the right questions? Did we search in the right places? Does his alibi really check out, or is someone lying for him? What could we have done to check this guy out further?

6 P.M., January 27

Three dead bodies lay on gurneys next to one another.

The friend who picked the wrong time to visit.

The mother who stayed home to baby-sit.

The son who never made it to the snow.

Two county pathologists, Drs. Pierce Rooney and Joseph Masters, began their tasks after working hours. Each no doubt had plans at home that Friday evening, but they stayed nonetheless. There was nothing routine about these deaths, and the pathologists knew how hard-pressed we were for evidence and suspects. So they went to work.

Dr. Masters started with Jason Miroth, determining that the boy had died of a head wound. Actually, he had been shot twice. The first bullet entered in the left temple region, three inches above the left ear. The pathologist noted that he believed it to be a contact wound caused by a gun held against the skull. That slug, a .22-caliber, was removed by Dr. Masters from the back of the boy's skull. The second shot entered the lower portion of the back of the skull and exited through the neck. The cause of death was brain damage from the first wound, which had been a coup de grace similar to that fired into Teresa Wallin. There had been no other marks to the body.

Daniel Meredith was shot twice, too, first in a between-the-eyes shot that entered between the eye and nose on the right side and pierced the brain, exiting in the back of his skull. The second shot entered the left sideburn area and also went out through the back of the head. From the powder marks found on the skin it was determined that the gun had been held twelve to eighteen inches from the victim. Either shot would have been fatal. There were no other marks to his body either.

Evelyn Miroth was another matter entirely.

Dr. Rooney found that she suffered a single gunshot wound that entered above her left eyebrow, passed through the brain, and was recovered from the space between her brain and skull. Her right eye had been partially removed by cutting the muscles around the eyeball. The uniform cut would not be easy to do, and the doctor felt it was purposeful activity rather than a wild, slashing type of attack. Miroth also had multiple cuts on the neck and a stab wound above the left clavicle.

Turning his attention to her abdomen, the pathologist determined that the woman had been cut open by a nine-inch cut running from the margin of the rib cage on the left side to just above the navel. A five-inch cross cut went through it, just above the midpoint of the abdomen. The wound was wide open, with much bowel extending from it and dangling over the left side of the abdomen. Several of the organs inside the abdominal cavity had been stabbed, though there was no injury to the kidneys. The liver was visible, and a portion had been cut off. There did not appear to be any random stab marks around the abdominal area; the doctor specifically noted that the small intestine had not been cut. In his opinion, the attack was specifically directed at particular organs.

(In his examination of these wounds, the pathologist discovered a small piece of latex embedded in tissue. It was later determined that this material had probably come from a rubber glove worn by the killer during his attack. He evidently sliced the glove during his stabbing of the victim. We already knew that Wallin's killer had worn gloves. As at the Wallin scene, CSI investigators found suspicious "swirling" prints at the Miroth scene that they believed were left by rubber gloves.)

Later, when comparing these findings to the results of the autopsy done on Teresa Wallin, Dr. Rooney would note that essentially the same organs were cut and pulled from the abdomen of both women. Such movement of the organs, he wrote in his report, "facilitate getting at blood in the abdominal cavity."

There was a new cruel twist introduced by the killer.

Examining Evelyn Miroth's rectal area, Dr. Rooney found a cut that extended from the back part of the rectum up the back of the buttocks. The uterus had been cut in six different places, and the pathologist believed this was accomplished by a knife thrust through the rectal wound.

In a rectal smear the doctor found a "great deal of sperm . . . consistent with a very recent ejaculation." He did not think the quantity found could have survived sexual activity from the night before the woman was murdered. (This note would be made to the file: Bill, the man Evelyn was romantically involved with, would tell investigators that they last had sexual relations on January 23 but had never engaged in anal intercourse. Bill did not think she was involved with anyone else, including Meredith.)

As the violence and depravity became worse, one thing became clear. The East Side killer was not going to stop.

Not on his own, anyway.

That late January I felt the lonely weight of singular responsibility bearing down on my shoulders.

The murders on Tioga Way and Merrywood Drive had been committed only two years after I had been assigned to head the Homicide detail. It was a job I wanted and one for which I hoped I was qualified. But I was wondering, for the first time, if I was up to the job.

A madman was on the loose in our county. He had wiped out three people for sure, and probably a fourth, on Merrywood this day. That, after killing doubtlessly twice before. So far he had remained unknown and undetected.

My job went beyond catching a killer. If our suspect went home and locked himself in his bedroom waiting for us to find him, our job would be difficult enough.

But clearly this man was not given to such self-imposed vacations. We had to stop him before he struck again. But we had failed to do so in time to save the lives of four human beings on Merrywood. How long did we have until he struck again?

The bloody ringlets, and the internal organs cut and ripped from his female victims' bodies, didn't give me a hint as far as the motives for the murders were concerned. It was an obvious call that the man hated women.

But beyond that, we couldn't conceive of what bizarre purpose motivated the killer other than some perverse curiosity about the bodies.

I suspected our killer would eventually be caught, and the case solved with the use of traditional homicide techniques—some of them basic methods as old as the work itself. Our people on the street would knock on as many doors and meet as many witnesses and suspects as possible. Patient detectives would eventually start getting the right answers to questions they'd asked a hundred times before.

Those distinctive shoe prints found in both the Tioga Way and Merrywood Drive crime scenes were not our only clues. Both scenes were loaded with signs of one sort or another, including bloodstains, fingerprints, shell casings, and the dead people themselves.

The truth was that there was enough evidence in the Miroth home to keep a full squad of technicians busy for two days. From the time Deputy Clark entered the home shortly after noontime until the technicians finished, processing the place for fingerprints, footprints, bloodstains, and a variety of physical evidence, the crime scene had been sealed off from all but a chosen few.

The shoe prints, though, would give detectives something to look for when talking to possible suspects. Most killers will hide their weapons but not think to change their shoes. Bloodstains, fingerprints, and shell casings could all, with luck, be tied to the killer. Laboratory procedures needed for comparisons of these shreds of evidence were not speedy operations. Time would be needed to examine and assess most of the clues we had collected. And even those diagonal shoe prints would have to be matched to suspect shoes submitted to the crime lab.

Such is the basic spadework of all murder cases. But once in a while murders are solved with the use of diverse and even exotic techniques.

I was willing to consider the exotic.

In 1976 I had attended a two-week school directed by FBI Special Agent Russ Vorpagel. The first week we heard about the basics—cuttings, slashings, strangulations, hangings, shootings, and the multitude of ways we have learned to kill each other. The second week was called the Psychology of Murder; it was fascinating. Instructors from the Behavioral Science Unit of the FBI were just beginning a program called "psychological profiling." Murders that were seemingly without motive often *did* reveal, we learned, psychological clues as to the type of person responsible. Many times the behavior and personality of killers are reflected in the crime scenes in the same manner that furnishings in a home reflect the character of the owner.

This was state-of-the-art crime-busting stuff, with only a minimal track record. But what did we have to lose?

Nighttime, January 27

Sergeant Habecker agreed with me we should give it a try. We made sure we each had a full cup of hot coffee, then shut the door to Homicide's cramped office.

Things had gotten crazy the past couple of weeks, with cops from other details sticking their heads in wanting to know if they could help solve our string of murders, or just idly curious and wanting updates.

To ensure no such distractions we pushed and shoved a heavy desk over to block the door. King Kong would have had a tough time bothering us.

First we discussed in a general way the crime scenes and the ensuing investigations. Then we became more detailed, throwing things back and forth at each other. Why did he do this? What about that? How do you explain this?

Dr. Pierce Rooney, who had autopsied most of the bodies, believed the savage attack on Evelyn Miroth was a "purposeful activity" rather than a wild, slashing attack. That would have us trailing not just a mad killer, but one following some sort of plan of attack.

We drew a circle on a map of the area that encompassed the Wallin and Griffin murders, the daytime burglaries, and the January 25th mutilation killing of a young dog.

Everything that had happened, *all the killer's activities* known to date, had occurred within the circle we drew. It was exactly one mile wide. We felt certain that our man was operating in his own backyard and was not a commuter.

So who was he?

Using generic profiling techniques I had learned at the FBI school, combined with gut feelings Habecker and I had about what we'd seen at our crime scenes, we made these assumptions about the killer:

- He was a white male in his twenties. Our reasoning was twofold: The area in question was primarily suburban white, and no suspicious black and Spanish males had come to our attention; also, the suspicious person "wanted for questioning" in our Crime Bulletin fit this description.

- He was probably schizophrenic. By definition his psychosis was characterized by withdrawal from reality and by highly variable behavioral and intellectual disturbances. Our reasoning: The attacks had occurred in the daylight, and there was no effort to hide the crimes or the evidence (expended casings, knives, etc.), though he obviously did not want to be caught because he left the scenes, and always undetected. This seemed to be another part of a fragmented mind intent on killing and mutilating regardless of the surrounding neighborhoods, where people had been moving and milling about.

- He was a loner, unmarried, and if working had a menial job at best. Our reasoning concerning his marital state: nothing specific, but who could live with an individual like this except his own mother? Regarding his employment, his attacks occurred during normal work hours during the weekdays.

- He had limited social skills and was not a con man or manipulator. Our reasoning: There was no prolonged interaction with the victims, no tying up or other movement in the house while the victims were alive. He was a stranger who seized an opportunity and made a blitz attack on his victims. He killed quickly in order to gain control of the situation.

- He could drive, but his main transportation to the crime scenes had become walking. Our reasoning: The Griffin killing was a drive-by, and he had stolen Daniel Meredith's car to flee the scene. But also, the bulk of the suspicious-person reports from East Area had a man on foot.

- He might have been recently released from a mental institution. Our reasoning: This seemed likely due to the type of crimes involved. Also, they had suddenly occurred within a short span of time in one area, as if he was a newcomer.

In short, we had profiled a weirdo who lived in the area he stalked and walked to and from the crime scenes.

Great.

Now all we had to do was catch the guy.

While Habecker and I were holed up in the office putting together a profile on the East Area killer, dozens of detectives and deputies were out on the streets, continuing to collect vital information. Early suspects and possible suspects were being eliminated rapidly.

As a matter of course, homicide detectives are inclined to examine carefully the backgrounds of families. Indeed, statistics reveal that seventy percent of murder victims know their killer. Next to husbands, former husbands are about as good murder suspects as can be found except for a person with a smoking gun or bloody knife in hand.

Vernon Miroth, Evelyn's ex-husband, in no way aroused our suspicions. Even the cause for the dissolution of their marriage had been pretty pedestrian, as such things go. No love triangle was involved, nor any violent lovers' quarrels.

On Saturday morning, the day after the Miroth murders, Detective Tom Carter took a call from a man named Ernest Slaving, who said he had been on his way to a bank located in County Club Centre the previous morning when he saw something that got his attention. A man driving an older-model Ford Ranchero or Chevy Camino—he wasn't sure which, but both are pickup-style vehicles—stopped and parked his car in a traffic lane facing Wells Fargo Bank. The man then got out and left his vehicle for several minutes, causing all the other traffic to have to go around him into the other lane. The plates on the vehicle, Slaving remembered, were from out of state —possibly with red lettering—"maybe Florida or South Carolina." When the man returned to his vehicle he drove off but parked nearby, adjacent to a dumpster at the rear of Liberty House. This report went, with all the others, into our bulging files, where it stayed buried.

We knew that fringe members of the Manson clan had been reported living in the Sacramento area. At the time, Charles Manson was serving his time in nearby Folsom State Prison. He was reported to be in daily contact with his followers. Not too long before that, Manson disciple Lynette Fromme had been apprehended in Sacramento's Capital Park during an attempt to assassinate then–President Gerald Ford. A number of concerned citizens called to suggest that members of the Manson clan might be responsible for the killings. Admittedly, there were some similarities between the Bel Air murders by the Manson clan and our killings, particularly the slashing and mutilation of the victims. Still, I didn't give much thought to this theory from our well-meaning amateur sleuths. We were convinced we were dealing with a lone killer, not a group effort.

It was almost noon on the twenty-eighth when Sergeant Jim Bevins took a promising call from a woman who believed she might have seen the red station wagon being driven by a suspicious person. He went out immediately to interview her.

She told Bevins that on the previous morning she had driven to a large department store, arriving shortly after 10 A.M. After shopping for a while she returned to her car. As she headed out of the center, prepared to turn left onto El Camino, a red station wagon pulled directly in front of her. Narrowly avoiding a collision, she remembered calling the driver of the wagon a hoodlum, based on his "crazed" looks and antics. The intersection where the near-accident took place: El Camino and *Merrywood Drive.*

Asked to describe the driver, she remembered he was a white man in his twenties with long, straggly hair. She didn't remember whether or not the man was bearded, nor could she describe his clothes.

At the time she was angry, but then she forgot the incident. Then she watched the evening news on television. She realized that she had been in the vicinity of the killings at about the right time, and that the red station wagon driven by the rude clod matched the description of the victim's car.

We were flooded with calls describing a variety of weirdos. Some of the people who reported strange incidents seemed to be making a good college try at getting rid of people they didn't like—or at least embarrassing them by subjecting them to a visit from the police. Others seemed sincere, and their information was easy to verify or discount. More often than not the "suspects" had been miles away in the company of others at the time of the murders.

One young woman could not make up her mind which of two "weirdos" was suspect. She leaned toward both. There were solid leads and some strange ones. We took a telephone call from a local resident who had moved to the area from Winding Creek, Utah. He remembered a murder there that he thought was similar to the East Area killings.

"The killer was a Theodore Bundy," he remembered. He said Bundy was a recent escapee from a Colorado prison. Our calls took us to El Paso County in Colorado, and then to Mel Blakley, a deputy D.A.

there. Blakley told us about Bundy, the smooth-talking sex killer (who was executed in 1989 for the murder of a twelve-year-old girl in Florida—the last of more than thirty young women he killed between 1973 and 1978). We knew all about Bundy by the time he was executed. But in 1978 we had never heard of him. He got our attention for a short time. In the end, the Colorado D.A. didn't think Bundy's modus operandi was anywhere near similar to that of our East Area killer.

And neither did we.

9

On the trail of the East Area killer we were making steady but too-slow progress. We would have benefited from some existing information if it had been readily available.

The records of a sporting goods store on Arden Way showed that a .22-caliber semiautomatic handgun had been sold in early December, 1977, to a man with a Watt Avenue address. He had waited the required fifteen days, then picked up his weapon on December 18, 1977—eleven days before the murder of Ambrose Griffin. He had also bought a box of ammunition.

Like everyone else who buys a handgun in California, Richard Chase had signed papers stating he had never been convicted of a felony, was not a mental patient, and had never been adjudged a danger to others as a result of mental disorder or mental illness. He also had to show his driver's license, and its number was duly noted.

On January 10 he bought more ammo—three boxes worth from another sporting goods store, this one located on Watt Avenue. As required, he had left his driver's license number for this purchase, too.

Technically, all this information was available to us and should have helped us find our killer. His purchases were, after all, a matter of record. Now let me tell you the hard realities. These records were literally buried among all the similar applications, files, and registrations made during the same period. There were thousands of people who lived in the one-mile circle who had made similar transactions. Unfortunately, handguns and ammunition were bought by lots of law-abiding citizens, too—particularly at Christmastime for presents.

We had begun our search back into the sales records of sporting goods stores starting with the first of December. But it would take time, a lot of time, and we weren't even sure it would net us anything. After all, the killer might well have brought his gun and ammo with him from another county, or even another state. To help us find a killer quickly and efficiently while he was still on the rampage, these records had little value.

Now, if the killer was using an Uzi or some other specialty weapon that could have been more easily tracked through legitimate gun dealers, that would have been different. But in picking a .22 the killer chose the most popular weapon for weekend target shooters from Maine to California. It is the cheapest to buy, and the ammo is inexpensive. It is often the first and possibly only gun that a father teaches a son to shoot.

The .22 is also, I should add, the weapon of choice for professional killers. A Mafia hit man will tell you it is the easiest weapon to silence. Even unsilenced, its "pop" is something that at a distance can easily be mistaken for a firecracker or backfire. (Our man had certainly killed silently, or at least quietly, with his .22—and in daytime, when people are up and about. According to the brass casings we found in the Wallin home, at least three shots had been fired there. No less than six bullets had been used to snuff out the lives in the Miroth home. And yet not a single gunshot was reported.)

Also, a .22 is more difficult to trace because there are so many of them—for years .22 guns were not even serialized by the manufacturers, except in lots of a hundred.

Why don't hit men use more powerful handguns, you ask, if they want to do the job right? Because you don't need a Colt .45 or .357 Magnum to kill someone if you are placing the barrel six inches away from your intended target. That close, the .22 has enough velocity to enter the body and bounce around inside, doing great damage. Often it doesn't have enough force left to exit. The cruel irony is that it can do even more damage than a higher-powered bullet that enters and exits the body cleanly.

Not far from the scenes of the East Side murders a young woman had settled into her new apartment. She listened to the news on television, read the local news accounts of the murders, and actually found herself wondering about the strange young man who had until recently been her neighbor on Watt Avenue.

Yes, he *had* been strange, Dawn Larson remembered. But she didn't really think he was a madman capable of doing those kinds of horrible things.

Once, in December of 1977, she had looked through his usually draped front window and noticed a large map hanging on the wall above a couch. It looked to her like a map of Sacramento. It also looked as if it had been marked in several places with heavy black ink. Had he been looking for work? she wondered.

She still thought once in a while about the animals he had taken into his apartment.

Many times she had seen Richard Chase take closed boxes from his apartment. Yet she did not connect them with the animals.

Not once during the time she had lived next door did she say anything to anybody about the young man. He behaved strangely, sometimes weirdly, but he had done nothing that clearly warranted reporting him. Besides, she hadn't wanted to make an enemy—not of *that* guy.

Our massive neighborhood canvas operations were our main weapon, but even at top speed that was slow, laborious work. Not only were we still talking to residents in the Wallin and Miroth neighborhoods, but we were now knocking on doors in the area where we had found Daniel Meredith's car. In all, at any one time at least fifty detectives were out pounding pavements.

Slowly—I hoped to heaven not *too* slowly—we *were* putting together a profile of the killer and had narrowed the territory where we thought he lived and operated. I did believe we were getting closer to him all the time. But would it be in time to save lives?

We examined and reexamined our evidence. Several men judged by witnesses to be in their twenties or early thirties could be classified as suspects. One woman had temporarily been on the suspect list because her personality edged toward violence, but she had been dismissed.

But at least nine people who lived in the Wallin and Miroth neighborhoods had focused their attention for at least a short time on a suspicious young man whose appearance and behavior was different enough to form a permanent impression on their minds. According to the common description of the man, he was fairly tall, skinny, and dirty, and he wore a filthy orange jacket. We had made him, of course, the subject of our artist's sketch.

It sounded like people who had seen this dirty young man were leading us solidly to the killer. There was one problem with that. They had described the man we at least wanted to question, yes. On the other hand, living and working in the metropolitan Sacramento area are about one million residents. There are a lot of skinny, scraggly, dirty young men among them. It would take a while to talk to them all.

We hoped our chore would not be quite that big. We believed we had isolated the East Area killer to one small, though thickly populated, area. But contacting everyone in that circle was still a big job.

Though I was heading this investigation I did not, of course, become aware of every bit of information as soon as a detective or deputy learned about it. Generally, the detectives who were canvasing tried to type their own reports before going home each day, in order to save time. However, these reports had to be signed by a supervisor, collected, copied, distributed, and assembled into a case file before someone in Homicide could glean any information. I guess we have our own trickle-down theory in police work. Other detectives, and usually all those in Homicide, dictated their reports into a tape recorder, then turned them in to be transcribed. Of course, during a major investigation the transcribers were overwhelmed.

Most of what I learned in the weeks between Wallin and Miroth came from verbal communication. Anyone who had come across something interesting would call me, rather than putting me in the position of having to wait for a report to surface.

I view my job, in such an investigation, as one of cheerleader and traffic cop. I was there to keep everyone convinced we would catch the killer by keeping the pressure on in the area and banging on doors. Once a street was covered I encouraged the officers to move on, but also to go back soon to catch the people they had missed on the previous block.

Don't ask just about what was unusual, I told the canvasing detectives, but ask about what is routine. Oftentimes it is easier to identify the latter, then point out where it varied, than to pull out something "unusual." Too, people will make observations during their normal routine that mean nothing to them but may have great significance to a cop working the case because he has more pieces of the puzzle.

Out there on the streets and in the homes of our

Sheriff's deputies look for evidence at the home of Ambrose Griffen on the night of his murder.

People's Exhibit #5: The home of newlyweds David and Teresa Wallin on Tioga Way.

People's Exhibit #4: In the brutal murder of Teresa Wallin, a bloody trail led from the living room to the bedroom.

People's Exhibit #15a: Blood rings on the floor next to Teresa Wallin's body are believed to have been left by a bucket.

People's Exhibit #47: The suburban home of Evelyn Miroth and her family.

People's Exhibit #51: The red station wagon belonging to Daniel Meredith where Richard Chase abandoned it—in a parking lot by the Sandpiper Apartments.

Evelyn Miroth

People's Exhibit #49:
Jason Miroth

People's Exhibit #52:
David Ferreira, the two-year-old nephew of
Evelyn Miroth.

VAN'S MARKET

BODY—DAVID FERREIRA

ARCADE WESLEYAN CHURCH

People's Exhibit #117: An aerial view of the alley in which the body of David Ferreira was found.

People's Exhibit #118: The box in which little David Ferreira's body was found.

Detectives Ken Baker (left), Wayne Irey (center) and
Bill Roberts discuss the case.

The booking photo of Richard Chase after his arrest in 1971 for possession of marijuana. Det. Roberts used this photo to compare Chase's physical appearance with that of the artist's sketch.

The police sketch of the suspect in the murder of Teresa Wallin that appeared on the back of a Special Crime Bulletin circulated by the Sacramento Sheriff's Department. This sketch appears as revised by Det. Roberts, who added the goatee and mustache.

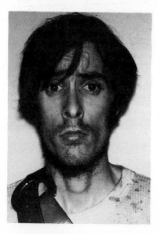

Richard Chase on the night of his arrest.

county were people who could solve our problem. People had certainly seen our killer entering or leaving the scene of one of his crimes, probably shortly after he had disposed of one of his victims. Whoever it was evidently did not have any idea about who or what he was or had been doing.

(Through the years I have never been able to understand how a man who didn't belong in the neighborhood could have entered the Miroth home and methodically killed a house full of people while the neighbors watched the place. Yet that, in effect, is what happened.)

The tenants in the Sandpiper Apartments, for example, gave complete accountings of their "normal" days' activities for December 27 and 28. Of course, to us those were not normal days, because we knew that our killer had, in all likelihood, left the car at the apartments, and in so doing he must have been seen by *someone.* Anyway, they told us when they left and returned, where they parked and walked, and what they had recalled seeing or not seeing. (Not seeing the red station wagon there at, say, 6 P.M. could be just as important as seeing it there at another time. We always are trying to narrow the window.) We would have them describe all the cars they remembered seeing in the lot and ended up with long lists of blue compacts, yellow trucks, and brown vans. Again, it was a matter of elimination.

As head cheerleader I reinforced the team's effort. By nature, cops, being civil servants locked into a bureaucracy, gripe and grumble about imaginary or real concerns that can only be changed over time. I have come to believe that such an attitude is healthy, as it shows the cop cares enough to want to make things run more smoothly. (Give me that any day over the cop who doesn't care and is too cynical to believe constructive change is possible.) But in the days that followed the Wallin murder every single detective and deputy working this case was *focused.* There was not a breath of griping or grumbling. Nobody was worried about advancement in grade or pay raises or the old coffee urn that had to be kicked a couple times before it worked. Rarely did I have to give orders in the military sense; mostly people found direction from our general discussions of what action needed to be taken.

"The baby's body could be in a dumpster," I told one group of officers.

Thereafter every dumpster and trash bin encountered behind a store or apartment house or in a parking lot was checked thoroughly by officers who gave no thought to how soiled their clothes might get. In some cases trucks were called in to turn the dumpsters over so that the trash could be hand-searched. Many a detective entering Homicide in those days was engulfed in what could only be described as a fetid, earthy aroma.

The traffic-cop part of my job was more difficult. To keep track of the direction of the investigation Sergeant Habecker and I used "lead cards," which were three-by-five-inch cards with a carbon flimsy attached. The hard-card copy of the lead (e.g., Check with Animal Control, Call lab about blood work, etc.) went into "Working Leads," and the assigned detective took the flimsy. Obviously, we needed to know just who was doing what at any particular time. If we got in some new information that changed the nature of the lead, then we were able to call that detective and brief him.

This was a simple solution to my constant fear that we might be overlooking something important. Granted, some of the cards I filled out were nothing more than ideas that I wouldn't even assign unless things got slow. But at least everything went down on paper, where all of us in Homicide could look at it and ruminate.

In the beginning, one of Don Habecker's assignments was to read each piece of paper that came into Homicide. It turned out to be an impractical assignment from the start and quickly broke down as information flooded in from the scores of detectives and deputies combing the East Area. In addition to this assignment Habecker was working on all three recent murders—Griffin, Wallin, and Miroth—plus one of our "unrelated" homicides. Since the paperwork came to us in stacks a foot high, and since there were only twenty-four hours in the day, verbal communication became *the* system for managing the case. This worked in all sorts of ways—standing in the hallway, huddled in the street, even over urinals.

The investigation became a real hip-pocket affair, with the hours long and the movement constant. The food staples were old, strong coffee and crackers pocketed from the breadbasket at your last real restaurant meal six or eight hours earlier.

Our basic philosophy and unofficial slogan was:

Keep Doing Something and We'll Smoke This Guy
Out.

We had received lots of attention, as such cases
usually did, from the local newspapers. Coverage of
the murders, including photographs, was detailed and
the headlines sensational, often carried on page one.

> **"Housewife Slashed to Death"**
> **"Who Killed Terry Wallin?"**
> **"Triple Murder in East Area—**
> **Baby Believed Kidnapped"**
> **"Three in Family Slain Here"**
> **"Madman Strikes—Three More Die"**

The account of Evelyn Miroth's murder noted the
similarity between her killing on Friday and that of
Teresa Wallin on Monday the same week.

Bill Miller, who handled our press relations at the
time, told about David Ferreira and mentioned that
he had been taken from the crime scene. "Missing and
presumed abducted from the crime scene," Miller was
quoted in the news. But newspapers weren't often
kind. In the next paragraph the story quoted Miller as
saying "there's not a great deal of hope he will be
found alive."

That was the ugly, brutal truth—the work of the
killer, not the newspapers that published the accounts
of David Ferreira's disappearance and probable
death. Still, my heart ached for his parents. I could
only imagine the pain they must be enduring—the
pain of their baby's loss, and the pain of not knowing
what happened.

A map of the area was published, reminding everyone how close the homicides were to each other. Merrywood Drive was one block from the southwest corner of the Country Club Centre parking lot. Tioga Way was next to the northeast corner of the Town and Country Village shopping center. The two centers were about a mile apart as the crow flies. Town and Country Village is located at the northeast corner of Fulton Avenue and Marconi. Country Club Centre is in the southwest corner of Watt Avenue and El Camino Avenue.

Daniel Meredith's sister, Hester Hull, who had introduced her brother to Evelyn, told the newspaper she had been a close friend of the murdered woman. Her brother, she mentioned, had said he was going to drop by and see Evelyn after he visited his doctor on the twenty-seventh—a plan that had cost him his life. He had left his sister's home at about 8:30 that morning to keep the date with the physician.

Like a lot of other people, she did not know of anyone who would want to kill Evelyn. She had known the murdered woman well, felt a bond with her because they were both divorced and made money at home with baby-sitting jobs. They had even obtained work for each other.

One of the news stories quoted then–Sheriff Duane Lowe as saying we were working around the clock on the case. He was right about that. Our detectives were becoming blue-bearded and red-eyed after endless hours on the job.

Among other things, we exchanged notes with the Sacramento Police Department. There, a retired man and his wife had been murdered without any apparent cause on January 12. But I could see no relationship between the crimes. I was told that their captain in charge of homicide was looking over our shoulders just as we had theirs. But the cases didn't seem tied together.

I found myself wondering almost hourly what kind of a madman we were chasing. There was no doubt in my mind we would catch him. The critical question was *when?*

And just how much more human wreckage would he leave behind before that happened?

10

January 28, 1978

At ten minutes to two on Saturday afternoon Wayne Irey was, to say the least, one tired cop. Irey, assigned to the East Side Rapist task force, had joined us at the scene of the Wallin murder five days before and had since been working Homicide day and night, mostly doing exhaustive canvasing. Before that he had been getting little rest while chasing the elusive rapist and putting in many long hours of overtime.

Irey, a stocky guy with sandy brown hair and a pronounced Kirk Douglas-like cleft in his chin, was a character and a good guy to have around. When he walked into the room it was always, "Ray, how the *hell* are you?" Then he'd methodically go around the room and give everyone else the same enthusiastic greeting and handshake. He was the type that most guys wanted for a partner because he was good-natured and had a sense of humor, in addition to being a good cop. A nice combination when you could find it.

I had just filled out a new lead card and was looking for a warm body to handle it. At that moment Irey ambled into Homicide, greeted those of us in the room as if he hadn't seen us in a month, and plopped himself in a swivel chair with what looked like a cup of hot coffee in his hand. With a grunt he put his feet atop a desk. He looked mighty tempted to take off his cowboy boots, but I caught him before he had a chance to do so.

After I handed him the lead card he smiled and said something about always being happy to find more work. Like so many of us, Irey was almost out of gas, but that didn't keep him from doing his job. And doing it well, at that.

Let me backtrack.

At 11:45 A.M. that morning Detectives Bill Roberts and Carol Daly, assigned to checking the background of various victims as to where they shopped and did various other errands, showed up at one of the East Area command posts set up to coordinate field searches and canvas team operations. They were told about a call that had come in from a sergeant in the county marshal's office. He had reported that his daughter-in-law had had a run-in with a suspicious man at a local grocery store on the morning of the Wallin murder. The woman, Nancy Holden, claimed she had gone to high school with the man, whom she had identified as a Rick Chase. It sounded pretty routine—very much like another possible dead end, but of course, worth checking out.

By phone, Roberts ran Chase's name through Motor Vehicles and obtained an address of 2934 Watt Avenue, Apartment 12. He also got his date of birth (5/23/50), height (5'11"), and weight (140 lbs.).

Then Roberts and Daly drove out to the apartment complex and knocked on the door of Apartment 12. A man who identified himself as Gerald Berringer (and had ID to prove it) answered the door. He said he had lived in the apartment only two weeks and did not know anyone by the name of Richard Chase. When they couldn't raise anyone at the manager's office Roberts and Daly left, not realizing, of course, that Chase, who had previously lived in Apartment 12, now lived three doors away in Apartment 15.

It had not been that big of a deal to Roberts and Daly, even though they were aware that Daniel Meredith's station wagon had been found very close by. Since that discovery detectives had been knocking on all the doors in the area, and they knew that a couple of possible suspects from the immediate area had already been questioned.

Daly went back to her fieldwork, and Roberts returned to the office, where he told me about the call. He decided to dig a little further on Chase.

In the meantime I asked Wayne Irey to call Nancy Holden and get any further details she might remember. I wouldn't have called it a hot lead. It was just the type of routine checkout we'd been doing for days.

Irey called her at 2 P.M.

As Nancy Holden, twenty-five, began telling of her run-in with her old high school classmate at the Pantry Market in Town and Country Village shopping center on the morning of the Wallin murder, Irey grew increasingly interested.

The detective asked her to describe Chase, and as she did he pulled out the description of the "suspect" we wanted for questioning in connection with the Bernece Street burglary—which we had sent out with our crime bulletin on the Wallin murder, along with the sketch.

Holden said: "Well, Rick is white, almost six feet, very slender build. His hair is dark brown, over his eyes, collar-length. He wasn't clean-shaven but appeared to have more whiskers on his neck than on his face."

Irey read from the bulletin: *white male adult, early to mid twenties, 5' 10" to 6'0", slim build, dark brown hair.*

"What was he wearing?" asked Irey.

"Let's see," she said, pondering a moment. "A bright orange ski parka, blue Levi's, tennis shoes."

Bulletin: *blue Levi's, black tennis shoes, orange jacket.*

Why had she waited five days after the incident to call now? Irey wanted to know.

She explained that she had gone to visit her in-laws that morning (Saturday) and a sheriff's deputy happened to be visiting her father-in-law. She had parked right behind the sheriff's patrol unit. As she walked past the vehicle she happened to glance inside. On the front seat was the artist's sketch of our burglary suspect. She recognized the "very strong resemblance" to Rick Chase, and once in the house she told father-in-law and the deputy about the Pantry Market run-in, and they encouraged her to report the incident.

"Will you come downtown? I'd like to talk to you some more about Richard Chase."

Right away, she said.

Yes, hard work *is* what makes or breaks any major homicide investigation. But I never said that a little luck along the way doesn't help.

Late afternoon, January 28

Bill Roberts ran Richard Chase's name through our Records Section and came upon his arrest on a concealed weapons charge in 1973 for carrying a .22 handgun, and for being a missing person at American River Hospital in 1976. In the latter listing he was described as being a "violent mental patient." The record also revealed that Chase had been a suspect in a 1968 shooting. Further arrests—in 1967, 1968, and 1971—were for possession of marijuana.

Roberts also found information on Chase's 1977 Pyramid Lake arrest. By calling the Department of Justice he was able to come up with the address Chase had given at that time: the same Watt Avenue street address, but Apartment 15. Christ, Roberts thought, three doors away.

Roberts found an old booking picture of Chase, who at the time had a mustache and goatee. The detective got a copy of the sketch of our clean-shaven suspect. With a black marker he drew in the same facial hair on the suspect, and he put them side by side. The similarity nearly took his breath away.

By now Irey, finished with Nancy Holden (who identified our artist's sketch as Rick Chase), was also convinced that Chase might be the East Side killer.

They were both flying high now, fueled by their own adrenaline and feeding off each other's excitement.

I should point out that Irey and Roberts, having been detectives for only two months, were still rookie detectives (but *not* rookie cops).

"We've got him!" Irey told me excitedly. "This is our killer! There's no question in my mind."

Detective Roberts, having been out once before to try to talk to Chase and, since then, coming up with a record that involved guns, shootings, and mental-hospital stays, was just as enthusiastic.

Chase *did* look like a good suspect, sure, but that was all he was as far as I was concerned. I had been through scores of possible suspects who, one way or another, could prove they had nothing to do with the murders. Maybe I was a little down because we had already cleared two "weirdo" surefire suspects that very day.

"Just go out there and see if he'll come downtown for an interview," I suggested. "If he won't, see if he'll give you a statement there."

If the tone in my voice had registered, they would have received this subliminal message: Easy does it.

Another new detective, Ken Baker, happened to be in the office. Irey and Roberts recruited him to join them, though Baker wasn't keen on the idea. He sincerely thought he had better leads to check out. He was nearly dragged out of the office by his two colleagues.

All three of them had already banged on many doors in the Watt Avenue area during canvas operations after the station wagon had been found at the Sandpiper Apartments. Undoubtedly someone had been at Chase's door. (We would later find out that the door of Apartment 15 had been knocked on more than once, though never answered.)

So I had no reason to be certain that we'd found our murderer. But if I had thought so, would I have gone myself to the Watt Avenue apartments that afternoon?

The answer is no. I fully accepted my role as cheerleader and traffic cop. There is no way I would have tried to snatch any of the glory away from detectives who had busted their butts on the case. If there was an arrest to be made that day, these detectives would make it, and I would be the happiest homicide inspector in the country.

There are times in some people's lives that are unique and provoke a rare emotion that is located somewhere between ecstasy and agony. Not everyone is so fortunate.

This feeling is related to fear, I believe, but it's not exactly fear. If it's curiosity, it involves an extreme amount. Courage is part of the equation, but the person involved is not aware of his bravery. Actually, the feeling is more like being caught up in an event that cannot be avoided, yet is far from accidental.

This feeling comes to people in a variety of ways and under scores of circumstances. High school football players have it when they are lined up on the field seconds before the opening kickoff. Boxers know the feeling as they are being given final instructions by the referee before round one and hearing nothing but the blood pounding in their eardrums. Marines feel it as their assault craft creep through the darkness toward an enemy shore and they know they're seconds away from the thunder and growl of guns that will canopy the sky with chunks of molten steel.

Violence will explode around them momentarily, and there is no way to get away from it except to turn their backs and run away. But that would be worse, much worse, than facing it—and winning.

Frankly, it's a feeling most "normal" people don't want too often in their lives, and yet there are others who desire its addictive powers or they would not enter boxing rings or join the U.S. Marine Corps or become cops.

When it finally comes, these people may marvel at why they let themselves in for this moment of danger. But that is quickly dismissed. Those who have chosen to put themselves in this position will act automatically. They will respond to their training, make the right moves, do the right thing, and all the while, hardly know why.

At 5:45 P.M. the three detectives parked their two unmarked cars in front of the Watt Avenue apartments and entered the complex. They went directly to the manager's office, and this time they found Betty Tietjen home.

They were doing what they had done many times before. Still, that feeling was growing, the mysterious exhilaration and excitement any good policeman feels when mystery and danger are right around the corner.

Yes, Richard Chase did live there, Betty Tietjen said. Apartment 15. "Just below, on the ground floor."

Her tenant had lived in the complex for a while now and was quiet. There were never any complaints, and he never caused problems. She did pass along that Chase had been seen by other tenants carrying a rifle. There had been at least two such reports. There was no law against owning firearms, nor were there any apartment rules forbidding them. All the manager could do was warn him to be careful and not alarm the other renters. He had agreed to do so.

Tietjen also said she had spoken to Chase's mother, who paid his rent the first of every month, and that the older woman had admitted her son was a "victim of LSD abuse" some years back and that he was currently having some mental problems caused by his drug use.

The manager reported that her tenant and his mother were not presently getting along well, which was putting it mildly. Chase would only speak to his mother through the closed door of his apartment and would not let her in.

None of the facts the manager revealed did anything to calm the adrenaline rush the three deputies were feeling at that moment.

First they checked to see if Chase's car was parked in its space, and Tietjen confirmed it was. One of the detectives wrote down this description: 1966 Ford Ranchero, Florida license #1GK7986.

Then they allowed the manager to lead them downstairs and around to the outside walkway on the northern wing of the complex.

Though I have never asked them, I'm sure that each of those detectives experienced that feeling of imminence, with their breath getting shorter.

This was what it was all about: the moment of truth when you may have a very bad guy on your hands, and in the effort to bring him to justice your life may be put on the line. It's not something you've planned to happen today—not at all. If, as you finished your breakfast and kissed your wife and children good-bye this morning, you thought this might happen today, you would have lingered longer, hugged tighter, said some things you normally didn't. But now it was too late. You were on a collision course you had helped plot, and you would not turn back.

The detectives were fully alive, every sense on full alert, reaching peak performance and ready for any kind of action. Inside Apartment 15 was a man they believed to be armed. A man who might have committed multiple murders. A man who just might be a madman. There was a real chance that within seconds or minutes one of them would take a bullet from the man's gun and be wounded or killed in the line of duty. Still they moved forward. They were cops, and that was how they earned their living.

Apartment 15 faced north, on the lower level of the two-story structure.

The manager was saying that Richard Chase would probably not respond to knocking at his door. He rarely did. He was a "very private person," she explained.

The apartment, the officers noted, was located at one end of the complex, facing a narrow lawn area. The street was nearby—about seventy-five feet to the west. With no back entrance, the front door was the only way in or out.

Roberts knocked. "Sheriff's Department. We just want to talk to you, Richard."

Nothing.

One by one the detectives took turns knocking and calling out. Each knocked a bit louder than the others.

No matter how they felt, whatever their feelings about danger and excitement, the detectives were calm, almost detached while they continued their knocking and calling out firmly to Richard Chase. There was still no answer, or any indication that he was coming to the door.

Though the manager had a passkey, the detectives did not want to use it—not yet, anyway. They were keenly aware that if this was their man, and if they entered without permission and found incriminating evidence, the entire ball of wax might be thrown out of court because they did not have a search warrant.

Eventually the manager announced that the apartment adjoining Richard's was empty. She suggested one of them could listen against the wall for any noise coming from Chase's place. She produced the keys and opened the door.

Detective Baker entered the unit and put his ear to the common wall shared by the two units.

Outside Irey and Roberts waited tensely.

Baker came back out, saying he heard sounds from Chase's apartment. He could hear someone walking around in what he thought was the living room area. If Chase was not in the apartment, Baker concluded, someone else was.

They held a quick war council. It would be easy to

kick the flimsy door down, but these were smart, thinking cops, not cowboys. They had no intention of doing anything to contaminate any future legal case.

They went back to calling and knocking on the door, telling Chase they knew he was inside and they just wanted to talk to him.

"Look, one of us has to go back to the manager's apartment," Irey finally said. "Call Ray and ask him what he wants us to do—kick the door down or get a warrant."

Roberts went off with the manager.

Outside Apartment 15 beads of sweat had gathered on the foreheads of Irey and Baker—and it wasn't a hot day. They could come up with no logical reason for Chase evading them except guilt of some kind. They waited as patiently as men can wait under the circumstances while the door remained ominously closed and silent.

Meanwhile, at the manager's apartment, Roberts decided first to try telephoning Chase. The manager gave him the number, and then she left to rejoin the watch outside her tenant's apartment.

After two rings a man answered weakly: "Hello."

"Hello, Richard?" Roberts asked.

"Who's this?"

"Bill. Is this Richard?"

"Yes. Do I know you?"

"Bill, remember? We met a while back."

Chase hung up.

Roberts dialed the number again, let it ring eight times, but this time there was no answer.

The detective stepped outside Tietjen's apartment and went to the balcony fence. He whistled softly.

Down below Irey stepped out from the side of the building.

"He's in there," Roberts said as quietly as possible. "I just phoned."

Irey nodded.

Roberts then went back in to call me.

Irey and Baker put their heads together and came up with a plan. Near the door to Apartment 15 they loudly discussed that they would leave and come back later. Then they split up, each covering an end of the walkway in front of Chase's apartment. Irey headed in the direction of the street, and Baker went the other way. They did not go far.

Several minutes passed.

Standing in the doorway of an apartment two doors down, Irey started getting the feeling that something was going to happen. It's a sixth sense all good cops develop. Their man was going to run—Irey felt it in his bones.

Irey rechecked the lay of the land. Down the walkway toward the complex, perhaps thirty or forty feet away, Baker waited in the doorway of the vacant apartment. Irey was in the same position to the opposite side and was near enough to hear, now, unmistakable sounds from inside Chase's apartment.

Suddenly, the door to Apartment 15 opened.

Richard Chase, carrying a cardboard box, stepped outside. He shut the door behind him.

Chase started to head back to the rear of complex, undoubtedly in the direction of his car, when he spotted the solidly built Irey in the doorway of Apartment 14.

"Stop!" Irey ordered. "Sheriff deputies!"

Chase had other ideas. Rolling his eyes in shock, he swung around in the opposite direction and headed for the street, with Irey in hot pursuit.

Chase's flight was headlong into what he must have perceived as an empty walkway. He was in high gear, headed for Watt Avenue, and in full flight by the time he reached the point where the detective jumped in his way. At that point Chase threw the box at Baker, who deftly swiped it away.

It was then the track meet stopped.

Baker, a practical man, had already removed his .45 from his holster. He used the heavy weapon as a club as Chase ran by. His blow was short, swift, and sure.

Chase dropped to the ground so swiftly Baker thought maybe he had killed him. But the suspect rose quickly, came up to his knees, and was ready to hop up and resume his flight. At that moment Irey, bringing up the rear, came flying through the air and pounced on him.

The deputy was surprised at the strength of the skinny fugitive, who squirmed under him like a boa constrictor. As they wrestled Irey felt a solid lump under Chase's armpit. A handgun!

Perspiration dripped from Irey's face and collar and rolled down his back. Without hesitation he reached for his .38 and pulled it from its holster. Putting the barrel solidly against the side of the fugitive's head— "screwing it in his ear," as cops like to say—Irey hollered, "Stop or I'll blow your brains out!"

But Richard Chase had no intention of stopping his struggle. He continued to writhe and wriggle, fighting to break free. There was no question in Detective Irey's mind of what Chase would do if he could get either arm free. He would go for his weapon and try to take him and Baker out.

Irey wasn't ready to fire, of course. So while holding on tightly to the suspect with one arm and his powerful legs, Irey stretched his arm out and placed his .38 on the ground as far out of reach as possible. It wasn't exactly a textbook move taught at any police academies, but unless he *was* ready to blow Chase's brains out, Irey desperately needed both hands to win this fight.

Irey knew where Chase's gun was located, and getting to it was his first priority. It was a struggle for Irey trying to reach the gun while keeping the fugitive's flailing hands away. There was no doubt in the detective's mind that the weapon was loaded and that the suspect knew how to use it. Beyond anything else he had to keep Chase's hand off that gun.

Irey then noticed that the suspect alternated between reaching for his gun and trying for his hip pocket. The detective wondered what it was in that back pocket that Chase wanted so badly. What could be so important now?

Baker, meanwhile, was involved in a fight of his own. He was trying to pull at least one of Chase's arms out of the pile so he could slap handcuffs on his wrists. He finally succeeded in getting the thick metal bracelet around one wrist, and as soon as he did he wrenched Chase's arm just as hard as he could. He would have liked to have pulled it from its socket. As he did, and with this great new leverage, he went for the second wrist.

Irey knew that one of Chase's arms had been taken away from him, but there was still a second one, and there was that menacing lump beneath Chase's arm, still Irey's first priority. He wanted it so badly!

Finally Irey's strength and force of determination prevailed. He got to Chase's handgun and yanked it from its holster.

Baker, meanwhile, was forcing the fugitive's forearms together, inch by agonizing inch, so he could enclose those stubborn wrists with the handcuffs—

Snap!

It was the sweetest sound Irey had ever heard.

Both of Chase's arms were now pinned behind him by the strength of steel.

Almost casually now, Irey handed Baker the suspect's gun. Then, grasping a handful of hair in one hand and one of the suspect's arms with the other, Irey gave Richard Chase a powerful jerk, pulling him to his feet.

The manager had seen the struggle and hurried back to her apartment, where she told Roberts, who was still on the phone with me, "Hurry, your partners need help!" He relayed the message and hung up.

Roberts sprinted to the other side of the complex, where he was relieved to see everything was under control.

Irey hadn't let go of his pale, handcuffed prisoner. "He tried to run," the detective said, "but he got all worn out. Tell Ray the suspect is in custody."

Roberts quickly returned to the phone to let me know the suspect had been apprehended, but I was no longer at my desk. I was en route to Watt Avenue.

I can't remember ever having gone Code 3 (with red lights and siren) when traveling to see a captured suspect. As I said, time is usually on our side. I wasn't so worried about the suspect getting away from the three detectives (in fact, I soon received the message that he *was* in custody), but my mad dash now was to get there before the press and other bystanders started choking off the area. I wanted to be sure we got our guy out of there, fast and safely.

When I first set eyes on Richard Chase, who by then was in the back of a patrol car parked in front of the apartment complex, I was surprised at how skinny and undernourished he looked. But he seemed aroused by terror, too, not unlike a wounded wild animal. I had no doubt he had been a tough adversary.

I couldn't help but notice that our suspect was wearing a bright orange ski jacket, and that it was covered by dark brownish-red stains.

The prisoner's shoes, we observed, appeared to be covered with blood, as were his belt and trousers.

The handgun taken from him was a .22 semiautomatic pistol with a fully loaded twelve-shot clip. The barrel was blue steel, and the handle was wooden. There were stains on the handle and barrel. We all thought it looked like blood.

Irey, without comment, showed me what he had found in Chase's back pocket. It was a tan wallet. I opened it up, and the first thing I saw was Daniel Meredith's picture on a driver's license!

The wallet also contained a MasterCard, an auto club card, and Union 76, Mobil Oil, and Bullock's charge cards, all made out to Daniel James Meredith. He was also found to be carrying pictures of Jason and Evelyn Miroth.

In addition, Chase was carrying a pair of rubber gloves (large) with what appeared to be dried blood on the fingers, along with a partially empty box holding .22-caliber ammo and a key ring containing sixteen keys.

The suspect had strewn some of the box's contents on the ground. There were pieces of bloodstained paper mixed with crimson-splotched rags.

"Let me go," Chase hollered from the backseat to no one in particular, but to all of us. "I haven't done anything."

"Take him out of here," I told the patrol deputy. "I'll follow."

The patrol car was better equipped for transporting prisoners than our unmarked detective vehicles. From his rear-seat "cage" Chase didn't do much talking on the way—a little bit to himself, we heard later. The two things the deputy driving was sure he said were, "My apartment is a lot cleaner, isn't it?" and "I didn't do anything in my apartment except kill a few dogs." The deputy never responded, of course.

As the patrol car carrying Chase pulled away, escorted by two detective cars, I looked over my shoulder and saw that the electronic press was arriving in force.

No one had yet entered Chase's apartment, and at that point a disagreement broke out among several detectives as to whether or not a search warrant was needed. A sheriff's lieutenant had shown up on the scene, and he became embroiled in the discussion, too. Just before leaving I was asked for my opinion.

"Look, we've got a missing baby," I said. "He might still be alive, who knows? I say go in."

I then headed for downtown, following the patrol

car that contained Chase. Roberts was also in the patrol car, with Irey and Baker following me.

After some further hemming and hawing at the scene, I would later hear, it was agreed they should enter Apartment 15.

Habecker and Homen arrived and took charge of the crime scene. The apartment was searched and found to be filthy, but the missing baby was not there.

When we arrived upstairs the place was jammed solid with detectives waiting in the division. Word had gotten out, and those not assigned to the Chase apartment search had come in. These men and women who had worked so hard the past days and weeks were just standing there in that long and now quiet room, waiting. Waiting to see him.

Some of the detectives even climbed on desktops to get a better look. I had never seen a roomful of cops so quiet. We could have heard the proverbial pin drop.

Richard Chase, still manacled, passed in front of them on his way to a nearby interrogation room.

Chase was escorted by the three detectives who had made the capture. Between them, the three rookies had six months experience working Detectives.

None of the one hundred bone-tired detectives said anything; they just looked. Was this actually the man, they wondered, who was responsible for such evil?

Some time later, while everyone was still assembled, I had it in mind to give an articulate speech about how this department had risen to the occasion and done such a magnificent job on this case.

When I got their attention and the room silenced again I felt myself suddenly very emotional, and unable to push many words past the lump in my throat. All I could manage was: "I'm more grateful than I can put into words. I just want to thank you all. Everyone did a helluva job."

Later that night the detectives who had remained in the building, chewing the fat about the East Side Killer investigation, were cleared out in one fell swoop with the ring of the telephone and this report from Communications: The East Side Rapist had struck again, his twenty-ninth attack.

Police work is like that.

It never ends.

11

We all hoped Richard Chase would agree to talk to us after we read him his rights. If he did, it could be an important opportunity. A confession would tie up the case quite nicely. But sans a confession, Chase might well incriminate himself in the murders. Everything he told us, of course, could be used against him in court.

Wayne Irey and Bill Roberts came into my office and asked who was going to interview the suspect. They both assumed it would not be them, but someone with more experience working Detectives.

I looked at them. They were no longer tired; their exhaustion had been put away for several hours. At some point, I knew, it would catch up with them big time, and they would deflate like popped balloons. But for now they were still flying high from the thrill of the capture.

"It's your collar," I said nonchalantly.

Irey and Roberts looked at each other in stunned disbelief.

"You want *us* to interview him?" one said.

"You sure, Ray?" the other chimed in.

They were giving me a chance to change my mind.

"Let me know how it goes," I said.

At 6:42 P.M. the two detectives entered the ten-by-fourteen-foot interrogation room where Richard Chase was waiting alone. First things first: Irey read Chase his rights from a small printed card. No screwups now.

At first Chase seemed confused.

Irey read them to him a second time, then explained a further point or two.

"Yes, I understand," the suspect finally said.

Chase was willing to talk.

Opening question: Had he killed a woman on Tioga Way behind Town and Country Village?

The suspect mumbled something unintelligible, then ended it with an audible "no."

"The other one I want to know about was on Merrywood yesterday," Roberts said. "I want to know if you killed a woman over there, a man over there, a six-year-old boy over there, and if you did something to a two-year-old boy. I need to know, Richard."

"Okay," Chase replied.

"Did you kill anybody?" the officer persisted.

"No, I never killed anybody."

When Irey pointed out that the crime lab would be able to make a comparison of the samples taken from the dried blood on his clothes with the blood of the victims, Chase became emotional, seeming to be on the verge of tears. But he stayed quiet.

"Look, we can talk this out," Roberts said soothingly. "But we have to know if you did it, Richard."

"My apartment's a lot cleaner, huh?" Chase said. When he changed the subject his nerves seemed to steel.

Asked if he had been in Country Club Centre in recent days, he told his questioners he had not done anything wrong, had hardly been out of his apartment, had not disturbed anyone, and had hardly talked to anyone.

One of the detectives inquired about his dash for freedom and his refusal to respond to their knocking and calling out his name.

"You ran away from us," Irey reminded him. "We'd been telling you we were the Sheriff's Department and we wanted to talk to you. But you ran from us. Why?"

Chase told the deputies he was half asleep at the time, and they surprised him.

Roberts pointed out that he emerged from his apartment carrying a loaded pistol in a shoulder holster, something he would hardly do if he was half asleep.

"I just woke up," he persisted.

"If you were half asleep, why would you load a bunch of bloody rags into a box and then come running out with it? You don't put a loaded gun in a holster when you are half asleep."

"No," Chase agreed. "But I got into a lot of trouble lately."

"I know you got in trouble," Roberts continued. "Let me explain something. We are not going to try to lie to you and tell you it's going to be better. So don't lie to us either, okay?"

"Everything works out better if everybody tells the truth, right?" Irey added.

Chase's answer was a noncommittal grunt.

"Don't you think I know what's in the box?" Irey said.

"I don't know," Chase answered clearly. "Just had some papers and garbage and stuff."

Asked where he had been at certain times on certain days, Chase acted confused. One time he said he'd gone to a fast-food restaurant and lingered there, and another time he wasn't sure of his whereabouts.

Both were days on which murders had occurred.

He denied visiting Town and Country Village on the day of his encounter with Nancy Holden. He also didn't remember being on Tioga Way that day.

In answer to a question about the blood on his shirt, at first he said that he didn't know how it had gotten there. Then he changed his mind. "It came from dogs."

"You killed dogs, didn't you?"

He nodded. His admission seemed to trouble him.

Irey told Chase more about the technology that helps solve crimes like murder and catch criminals with modern methods. He went back to the issue because it had seemed to upset Chase earlier. They were looking for anything to break through his seemingly thick hide.

Roberts continued on the same line. "We check for fingerprints and footprints, and we collect blood, shell casings," he explained. "We have ways in the crime lab to compare bullets and blood and other evidence, you know. You will be surprised. They are so good nowadays that they can even take that shirt you got on and take the dried blood and compare that with the blood of one of the people who got killed. Did you know they can do that? They can do that with all those rags that are in the box you were carrying out of your apartment and find out whose blood that is. And I don't see any sores on you, so I don't think it's your blood."

"We can take that gun of yours and shoot some bullets through it, and that way we can find out, too, if they are the same bullets," Irey added.

"I thought it was about the damn dogs," Chase muttered.

"No, we are not talking about dogs," Roberts said. "We're talking about people. About kids, too."

"Now, I want to tell you something else," Irey said. "Remember when I found the gloves in your pocket? There seems to be blood on those gloves. Gloves leave prints too, did you know that? We have glove prints from the crime scenes, so we'll be able to compare your gloves with the prints left where the people were killed. You probably didn't know we could do that.

"We've got your keys here, too," Irey went on. "Let me ask you, Richard, are these your keys?"

Chase's grunt was affirmative.

"We'll check these keys, and we'll find out if these are your keys or if the keys belonged to somebody that got killed. Like does one of them fit a red Ford station wagon that belonged to one of the people that got killed? We are going to find all this out because we think you killed all those people, Richard. Now, it can be hard and will take time to do all this stuff, and we are going to keep you here while we do it, or you can make it easier and go ahead and tell us everything. We want you to tell us about it. Make it easy on yourself. I think you'll feel better after it's all over."

But Richard was not talking. "I haven't done anything, honest."

He was willing to talk about dogs.

"I brought in a couple of dogs. That's all."

"Into your apartment?"

"Yes," Chase replied. "And one got killed."

He admitted to shooting one dog, then to killing "several" dogs.

A confession is a confession. Hoping the suspect was in the mood for more, the detectives quickly guided the subject away from dead dogs back to dead humans.

"Why did you kill that little boy?" Irey asked him abruptly.

"I didn't kill any little boy."

"If you didn't, where is he, then?"

"I didn't see any little boy," Chase objected.

Roberts explained slowly, as if speaking to someone who didn't already know the facts, that on Merrywood the day before "a lady and her six-year-old son—and by the way, you were carrying their pictures" were murdered, along with a man, Daniel Meredith, "whose wallet you had."

"Richard, we know you did it," the detective said. "I just want to know why, what made you do it."

"I just . . . I don't know. I don't understand how it could be me," Chase stammered.

"You don't understand how it could be you?"

"No, I've done nothing like that."

"Are you a liar, Richard?" Irey asked.

"I've always told the truth."

"Always?"

"Almost always," Richard Chase replied.

Watt Avenue

As evening began to close over the city a fog moved in, and the weather turned damp and clammy cold.

Rope barriers blocked off the sidewalk entries to the north side of the complex. Apartment 15 was the center of activity.

Habecker and Homen were the first to enter the apartment. After a quick and unsuccessful search for any sign of the missing baby they settled in for a more careful inspection. Everything of interest they found was photographed, labeled, and boxed as possible evidence.

Richard Chase had left his apartment in complete disarray. A strong, putrid stench was the first thing noticed by anyone stepping inside. Almost everything in the apartment was bloodstained. The bedroom floor and bed. In the bathroom, the tub, walls, and floor. The front room and kitchen floors.

Crime scene investigators and technicians eventually followed the detectives to the apartment.

A sleeping bag covered the surface of a couch in the front room. A half loaf of French bread was lying on the couch, which was stained with blood. A round hole suspiciously resembling a bullet hole had pierced the ceiling above the bed. Two pictures showing different views of the human anatomy were on the wall, and under them the rug was liberally stained with blood.

An unwashed dinner plate was lying on the bed. It, too, was bloodstained, as was most of a pile of clothing that was also lying there. Three .22-caliber bullets were found on the floor, plus one expended round.

In the bathroom more bloodstains were found on the door, the floor, and the walls, and in the tub. A plastic drinking glass was discovered in the medicine cabinet. The glass was stained on the inside with blood.

In the kitchen, a can with a label indicating it had once held some kind of nutrition product was taken from the freezer compartment of the refrigerator. Several small pieces of bone were found in various areas of the kitchen. On the countertop was an electric blender; the inside was stained and smelled bad.

Found among a stack of miscellaneous personal papers and books and other reading material (including newspaper articles about the recent murders that had paralyzed the city) were:

- two loose plastic overlays removed from a medical book entitled *Live Science Textbook.* They depicted the internal organs of the human body.
- an article from a magazine, *Saturday Review of the Sciences* (May 1973, pp. 22–28), entitled "The Evolution of Menace," which had been photocopied.
- a hardcover book, *Introduction to Psychology* by Ernest Hilgard, with various lines on page 54

underlined in pencil. The title of the article: "Understimulation."

- a copy of *Prevention* magazine, a magazine about various health topics. Chase's name and address were listed on the subscriber label.
- a library book, *Totalitarianism* by William Ebenstein.
- a classified ad section from the Sacramento *Bee* dated Dec. 23, 1977, with numerous ads for dogs for sale circled in pen.
- a loose-leaf spiral notebook with handwritten notes, drawings (a gun, a swastika, obscene pictures), and translations of German words. On one page Chase had signed his signature twelve times, adding: "My name is Richard Chase. I am a 01000 computer. I was sent here in the year 10,000."
- a yearbook from Mira Loma High School, Sacramento, class of 1966. A "Rich Chase" is pictured among the sophomore class. He is a smiling, clean-cut youth. Friendly notes from other students fill the front and back pages.

The interrogation continued.

Irey covered Chase's run-in with Bureau of Indian Affairs at Pyramid Lake. The detective wanted the suspect to think there was nothing he could hide. Irey carefully dissected Chase's complete arrest record.

Chase seemed to pass it off rather lightly.

Accused point-blank of killing both Teresa Wallin and the three people in the Miroth household, Chase blandly denied everything. He denied having left his apartment on either Monday or Friday. Reminded he had been seen by both a store clerk and a shopper on Monday, Chase decided he had been seen by two other people some other place. One was a black man who worked at a service station; the other he described as "a blond guy." But he flatly denied the encounter with a woman either in the Pantry Market or beside her automobile.

Shown a photograph of Nancy Holden, he was noncommittal. Then he was shown a picture of David Ferreira. For a moment, just the briefest instant, it looked as if Richard Chase was wavering. Tears welled in his eyes, and he appeared to be on the edge of crying.

"You ever see that little boy, ever see either one of these people? They're dead. See that lady, the one who lived over on Merrywood, and she, ah . . . let me put the pictures in front of you so you can see them. She was killed, as you can see, and so was this man. And here is the six-year-old boy, Jason."

Irey had put gruesome crime scene photos down on the table for Chase to see.

The detective paused, as if for breath.

"Now, here's a picture of the baby boy his mother gave us. Cute little guy, huh?"

"Yeah," Chase replied.

"He's not at the house. You know what we think? We think the killer took him. And we think whoever did this had a reason for doing it. What do you think?"

Chase seemed to be close to breaking again. "Uh, I can't, ah, I can't think of any reason why . . ." He let his answer dangle, unfinished.

"You can't think of any reason why?"

"Uh, I don't know."

"Maybe you can help me try to think of a reason," Detective Irey told him. "I've been, you know, we've been trying to think about that ever since that one lady got killed Monday over on Tioga, and we tried to think why anybody would do that. Go in and kill a nice lady like that, you know, and shoot her and then cut her open like that. I don't understand, but there must have been a reason for something like that. And then there was that other lady on Merrywood killed in the same way, and the kid and the man, and now the baby is missing and probably dead."

Chase had recovered. He was not going to break, not going to do anything to help.

Asked if he had been to a psychiatric hospital, he admitted to being in a "rest home" for a short time. He was there, he said, after being poisoned. He corrected that shortly to explain he had eaten some "bad rabbit meat."

"Now, we have this wallet here. Daniel James Meredith, he's the man that was killed. You had his wallet in your pocket. You took it from him when you killed him."

"That's not my wallet," Chase interrupted.

"I know. But you had it in your pocket. If you had it in your pocket, you killed him."

Chase's denials continued. He claimed he knew nothing about the murders.

"You don't remember doing it?"

"No," Chase said. He was nowhere near breaking.

"Do you know why you did it?"

"No, I don't remember doing it."

"You don't remember doing it? Why do you lie to me when I don't lie to you?"

"Because, ah, I just, I didn't have any problems until just now, I mean, ah . . ." Chase hesitated as if his thoughts hadn't taken him any further.

"Did she scream, Richard?" This question was asked in softer tones.

Chase made a sound, but not an audible answer.

"Did that little boy scream?" The detective's patience was worn thin.

"No."

"Did you really feel good when you killed that little boy, Richard? Did you really feel good?"

"No."

"Did you really feel good when you ran that knife up this lady's butt? Did you really feel good when you did that?" the detective asked, flicking a crime scene photo of Evelyn Miroth back in front of Chase.

Chase didn't display any emotion. He simply answered, "No, I didn't do anything like that."

"You did, Richard," the detective insisted.

It was very quiet in the room for a long moment.

"No, I—I—all I did was kill some dogs," he finally answered.

"No," Detective Irey went on. "You've done this, you killed Mr. Meredith, you got his wallet. Your gun is the same gun that killed him. The gun that was in your holster is the same gun that killed him. We'll be able to determine that, but I know it's true. So do you."

"That wasn't my wallet," Chase objected.

"I know it isn't. It is the *dead man's wallet.* The one

you took off him after you shot him in the head. This five-dollar bill was his, and that's probably his blood on it. Why did you cut her up so bad, why did you do that?"

"I didn't cut anybody."

"You cut them with big butcher knives. You shot them in the head, and then you cut them up, and then you took the knife and you rammed it right up her butt. Isn't that what you did?" the detective insisted.

"I don't have any strength like that."

"You sure do. And that little boy there, smiling for his momma, wasn't even two years old. He was only twenty-two months. That little baby right there, Richard."

The detective held up a photograph of David Ferreira so close that Chase actually flinched.

The interrogation had been relentless, but Chase had been as stubborn as his questioners.

"You *did* do it. You keep on looking at that lady right there"—pointing to the picture of the mutilated woman—"and tell me you didn't do it. Did she scream? Did she try and protect her little boy Jason?"

"I didn't see any lady like that at all," Chase insisted. "I was at my apartment all day."

"No, you weren't. You walked away from your apartment, the manager already told us that. You didn't go back to the apartment till later in the day. A lady saw you driving the man's car, the man you murdered, the red station wagon you drove off in. The one you took that little boy away in. Then they saw you driving that car, so you did do it, Richard. Why did you do it? Do you drink their blood?!"

The question, asked bluntly and suddenly, would

have shattered many people. Chase accepted it calmly with a calm answer. "No, I didn't do anything like that."

"Your shoes, do you see those? They're full of blood. Your shirt is full of blood. Your coat is full of blood. You're not innocent, Richard. You're guilty. You murdered five people."

Chase coughed.

"You brutalized them."

"Yeah, well, it must have been somebody else, because there's trouble in that neighborhood every day," Chase announced.

"What neighborhood?" he was asked.

"Where I live, people get killed all the time."

"Nobody's been killed there except for these people. They're the only ones. Monday, do you know what you did last Monday?"

When Chase said he didn't, he was told.

"You went over to a young lady's house who was twenty-two years old and you shot her in the head. Then you dragged her back to the bedroom and you stabbed her, and then you gutted her. Yeah, you did, Richard. Oh, yeah, you did, pal. And you better start telling us the truth."

"I told you everything that I did," he maintained.

Irey and Roberts had the suspect to themselves for almost two hours. Each came and left the room three times, though never leaving the suspect alone. We wanted him to keep talking, to get used to the feel of it, and, we hoped, to let down his guard.

The two detectives, as they came and went, kept me posted on their results and lack of same.

After two hours we decided to try another tack.

Irey and Roberts came out.

They were replaced by Pat O'Neal and Tom Robinson, "old-timer" detectives who had worked Homicide for years but were now on other assignments. O'Neal was smooth and professional in his interrogation style; Robinson was more instinctive and inclined to shoot from the hip.

At 8:30 P.M. O'Neal and Robinson entered the interrogation room and introduced themselves to the suspect. They brought with them cold water and hot coffee, and Chase partook of both.

They also brought in more crime scene photos, and these poses seemed to unsettle Chase.

"You killed that lady right there," Robinson stated, pointing to Evelyn Miroth's butchered body. "You did it, right there."

"My God, I did not," Chase replied emphatically.

The detectives told Chase they had found his footprints in the Miroth residence after the murders. They told him they had witnesses who had seen him in the area and some who had seen him at the house.

"Five people are dead, and you did it. Right here, you see it?"

In the explicit photograph the detective pointed to, Evelyn Miroth stared sightlessly. Her eyes were cold and dead. "Five people dead out there, you see it? You see that?"

There was no visible reaction from Chase.

O'Neal reminded Chase that there was blood all over his clothes.

Again Chase said he didn't have any idea how the blood got there.

"You been drinking that blood?" Robinson inquired. The question sounded more like an accusation than a query.

Chase said no, unconvincingly.

"Does blood taste good?" the detective asked.

The suspect wouldn't cooperate. "Oh, come on, man."

At 9:12 P.M. I entered the interrogation room.

After introducing myself I made a point of sitting down next to Chase, rather than on the other side of the table. I had been told he became nervous when someone invaded "his space," so I did just that.

I also knew that Chase had spooked when an attempt had been made to take off his shoulder holster. Since the suspect wanted it so badly, we had let him keep it on.

"That's a handsome holster, Richard," I said admiringly.

As I reached out to touch the holster Chase recoiled, but I didn't let that deter me. I pressed forward until my hand was on his holster. I caressed it.

"Very nice," I said soothingly. "I guess you'd like for us to let you keep it, huh?"

He nodded anxiously.

"Maybe we can work something out."

I went back over several facets of his life, and his responses varied from noncommittal grunts to clearly spoken denials.

His voice, I found, was surprisingly soft, though quite high-pitched. He wasn't just nervous, I could see, but *terrified* of the surroundings. Apparently he was surprised to be there, having to explain his actions. He must have believed he could keep getting away with murder.

He expanded his confession about the dogs, though. He now remembered killing an Irish setter near Folsom Lake and the two Lab puppies he had taken into his apartment.

Gradually I worked back to the one person that was in all our minds. Little David Ferreira. But Chase again claimed he didn't know anything about a baby.

"Richard, if you saw somebody walking down the street with blood all over them like that, what would you think?" another detective asked.

Chase hedged for a while, then said he was wearing an "old hunting shirt" he had worn for killing dogs.

"Why don't you like women, Richard?" he was asked.

Chase hesitated.

"Because of your mother? What did she do to you?"

Chase said he did like women, though he added that he didn't have a girlfriend at the moment.

When he mentioned having a sister I persisted on this line. "You don't like her either?"

I suggested that perhaps he had been criticized by the women in his family, and turned away romantically by other women, and that he couldn't get a girlfriend.

This line of questioning missed its mark, as Chase didn't take the bait.

His interrogators surprised him when they asked Richard why he had lost so much weight since his driver's license photograph had been taken the previous year.

"Are you eating much meat, Richard?"

Chase said he was. He said he had been on a diet of New York steak, but he modified that to "things from the store"—meaning the grocery near his house.

One of us observed that a lot of cats were missing where Watt Avenue and Marconi intersected and wondered aloud if that was the kind of meat Chase was eating.

Again, what about all the blood on him?

Chase told us he had thrown a dead dog out with the trash a week ago.

"Oh, the blood on you a week old?"

Chase started to speak, but I interrupted. "It's still red. That means it's fresh blood, not a week old. Tell me, why don't you like dogs?"

"I do like dogs," Chase protested.

"Why do you kill them then? I like dogs, and I've never killed a dog in my life. Couldn't help it, could you? Something driving you to it? Tell me about it."

"Well, I guess I wanted a dog," Chase explained. "I took it out and killed it up at Folsom Lake."

He was excited, maybe confused, but still seemed in no danger of cracking. He was obviously cautious in his answers, though at times he exhibited signs of stress.

He did relent again on the subject of the dogs, giving us some details about how he had used a machete on one. He cut up the animal because it was mean, he said.

Always the questions returned to the woman on Tioga, the murder victims on Merrywood, the missing little boy, and his own appetite for blood.

The session ended at ten minutes to midnight.

Chase might have been exhausted by his questioners, but so were they by him. He was reminded by a detective that he had been read his rights earlier. Among those he had waived was the right to remain silent.

The suspect nodded.

We had taped the entire five hours of interviews. In spite of our various tactics and changing of the guard, Richard Chase had—in our jargon—"held his mud."

There would be no confession.

"All right, Richard," I said, standing. "We're going to take you across the street to jail now."

I could hardly wait to take that damn holster off him.

Wayne Irey was exhausted as he rode the three floors down to the Sheriff's Department parking lot, climbed aboard his motorcycle, and headed for home.

He drove out Highway 160, but long before he was close to home he realized he had to get off the road. He pulled off at the Canterbury turnoff.

As he sat there, still on his bike, a montage of memories from the last six days raced through his brain. He remembered how the week had started on Tioga Way. He had not seen the body of Teresa Wallin lying on her bedroom floor with his own eyes, but he had seen the photographs of her, flat on her back, staring sightlessly. The look in her eyes haunted him at the oddest times. Never in all his life had he seen such fear and anguish on a human face.

Irey realized he was shaking.

He tried valiantly to keep one thought foremost in

his mind: Richard Chase was behind bars, and he would never kill again. It was over, all over.

But her eyes . . .

A wave of emotion surged through his body. He lifted a hand to his cheek and felt something wet and warm. Curious, he brought his hand down and looked at it.

The man who had captured Richard Chase, who had kept him from reaching his murder weapon, who had wrestled him into submission and then escorted him to a patrol car, couldn't believe what was happening to him at that moment.

He was crying.

12:20 A.M., January 29

After booking Chase into county jail and outfitting him in green jail overalls, Detective Mike Hash and I escorted him into the sobriety testing room, where we were met by duty nurse Bea Wolfertz.

Chase sat quietly as the nurse took scrapings from under his fingernails and as we assisted her in collecting hair samples from his head, body, and extremities. All of these samples would be turned over to the crime lab to be matched with evidence gathered at the various crime scenes.

But his demeanor changed when Wolfertz was preparing to draw blood from his arm. In the end we had to physically restrain the suspect.

It seemed Richard Chase was afraid of needles.

5 P.M., SUNDAY, JANUARY 29

This was the first day of what would be a long follow-up period, gathering the remaining pieces of the puzzle that would someday be assembled in front of a jury charged with deciding the fate of Richard Chase. For another six weeks there would be no days off for detectives.

Our psychological profile was not instrumental in catching the killer, but the training we received at the FBI school had greatly influenced the tactics we used during the investigation. The most important tactic was to stay focused on the area in which the killer operated and not to go off on wild-goose chases, wasting manpower and allowing the bona fide leads to cool off.

(When the Richard Chase case was finally closed the entire file was turned over to the FBI's Behavioral Science Unit. Through the years they have used it extensively as a classic example of a "Disorganized Offender." Perhaps in their zeal to validate this new tool for law enforcement, the claim was made that the case was solved *solely on a very detailed profile* that allowed us to narrow our search and find an individual matching the profile. But allow me to set the record straight: This case was solved by *spadework,* talking to enough people and getting important information out into the field. Detectives went to Chase's apartment to speak to him based not on the profile, but rather on the report of a witness (Nancy Holden) who placed him near the Wallin residence shortly before the murder; his previous arrest with a .22-caliber weapon;

and his strange behavior at Pyramid Lake. The FBI's claim, often repeated at training seminars and conferences around the country, is a disservice to one of the best week-long team efforts ever made by the Sacramento County Sheriff's Department, and to the many individual deputies and detectives who worked nearly around the clock that week.)

The phone rang late that Sunday afternoon in Homicide.

It was the number-two-ranking public defender in our county, Farris Salamy. He informed us that he had been appointed Chase's attorney, and from that moment on we were not to have direct contact with our murder suspect.

Indeed, we would never speak to his client again.

12

February, 1978

Deputy William Schneider had become obsessed.

He would not have used that word to describe his own efforts, preferring something more reasonable, like "focused." But "obsession" was the word Schneider's wife would later use to characterize his involvement in the investigation since the Miroth killings. One couldn't blame her, since she saw Bill working eighteen-hour days seven days a week for six weeks straight. He came home, really, just to take a hot shower and grab some shut-eye.

But Schneider wouldn't have had it any other way. He was looking for little David Ferreira, and he wasn't prepared to quit until he found the baby.

I had given him a couple of early leads on the missing baby to check out. But from then on something clicked inside of Bill Schneider, and he became a self-possessed cop with a mission. Soon, virtually every lead about the missing baby was funneled to him.

At the same time, some other deputies and detectives had backed away from this most unrewarding job. It involved finding, most certainly, the body of a murdered baby. And I wasn't the only cop who found child victims the most difficult to handle emotionally.

As usual, we had held back from the public some important details about the case. Our crime lab reported that in addition to blood found in the Miroth bathtub, human brain tissue was also present. And in the opinion of the experts, the tissue came "not from an adult." While we had not released this information, we had made it clear to David's parents that "physical evidence" at the scene strongly suggested their boy had been killed.

Schneider, of course, felt all those same churning emotions the rest of us did about victimized kids, and still he took on the assignment. Not surprisingly, he had two young children of his own at home—one a little older than David, the other a little younger.

Schneider, over six feet and thin, worked the Ferreira case without a partner, which was fine by him. He was a loner anyway and hadn't seemed to enjoy much the team spirit of the Special Enforcement Detail (what many other departments called SWAT). He was intelligent, quiet, and even, according to one former partner, a tad standoffish.

At 1:30 P.M. on February 1, 1978 Schneider showed up at the Watt Avenue complex with a dog handler and a floppy-eared bloodhound named Clyde.

The dog "scented" on some clothes of David's given

to Schneider by the boy's mother, and then, on the doorstep of Apartment 15, the search began.

Clyde headed through the complex toward the rear parking lot. He became excited at the fence that separated the lot from the Sandpiper Apartments. Schneider knew that the red station wagon had been found on the other side of the fence, and in all likelihood Chase had come over the fence with the baby's body. Clyde knew that, too.

The dog had already hit on the red station wagon *and* the Ford Ranchero, both in our impound lot. That suggested Chase had brought the baby home in the wagon and possibly taken him someplace else in the Ford.

Still, Schneider wanted to check out the possibility that Chase, possibly on foot, had dumped the boy somewhere near his apartment. So far, some of the things in our psychological profile had, in retrospect, been close—and one of the strongest traits we had identified was that the killer did everything within that one-mile circle.

The dog and two men went back and forth from the parking lot to Apartment 15 a couple of times, Clyde with his nose lowered, barely clearing the ground, and the long-limbed Schneider marching behind the dog and his handler.

After forty-five minutes or so the dog took a new direction, heading across the bridge above Chicken Ranch Slough, which ran underneath Watt Avenue. When they hit the west bank of the slough (on the west side of Watt) they were on the grounds of Del Paso Country Club golf course.

Clyde, his tail wagging, padded out onto the course and searched around the fairways with the gusto of a twenty-five-handicap golfer looking for a lost tee shot that "has to be here somewhere." But alas, he found nothing.

Schneider noticed on his impromptu tour of the golf course a small, lily-gilded lake off to the side of one fairway. For a golf course it was a sizable expanse of water, and it looked to be fairly deep.

"Look, Ray," he told me later that day, "I want to go back there and ask them to drain the pond."

The pond at the private club where annual fees ran as much as Schneider and I made in a year . . .

Just six days earlier, on the night of the Miroth murders, fifty officers had searched the grounds of Del Paso golf course for David Ferreira's body. At nine o'clock that night officers searching for the child had opened the lid of a garbage can on the country club grounds and found a child's clothing stained with blood. We started searching the grounds before stopping to compare the garments that had been found in the garbage can with a description of the clothes David's mother said he had been wearing when she delivered him to the Miroth residence that morning. (They didn't match, as it turned out.) As dawn broke a few officers who were reluctant to end the search still scrambled over the fairways and greens that soon became populated with well-heeled golfers backed up at tees. Needless to say, play was disrupted. Still, our presence there drew scant complaint from mostly understanding members. And now we wanted their pond.

"The dog was all around there," he went on. "It's

right next door to where Chase lived. I'll just feel better if we have a look."

"Go for it," I said. It was a no-brainer call.

The next day, when Schneider advised the Del Paso management what he wanted to do and why, they couldn't have been more helpful. The entire city knew we had a missing baby, and our citizens were willing to help.

It took nearly two days to drain the pond, turning it from a picturesque hazard in the midst of an exclusive course to a mud-filled abyss resembling a Louisiana swamp.

The baby's body was nowhere to be found.

Spring often comes early in California's long central valley. But during the drought years of '77 and '78 it came quicker than usual, with winter creeping out the back door long before anyone gave a thought to the vernal equinox or even Groundhog Day. Blue and some golden lupines would soon be blooming in the rolling meadows of our foothills. Golden poppies would sprout in the sunshine, and a variety of plants and weeds had started to grow prematurely during damp November, then through a dry December and a chilly late January.

For Schneider, the colorful ground cover took on a different meaning. It could hide things—not only a variety of hardware and junk, but more grim secrets. Was David Ferreira buried somewhere beneath the stunted canopy of leaves and grass stems that grew in the vacant lots, creek beds, and meadows surrounding the East Area?

A shovel had been found in Chase's Ranchero, and

testing had been conducted. There were no signs of blood, and nothing conclusive was found as far as soil types.

Still, Schneider did a lot of hiking, searching through thirsty weed beds for telltale signs of a recent burial, clues of secretive behavior, footprints, or some odd discarded item that might be connected to Chase.

Schneider even went to see Richard's mother, Beatrice Chase, just in case the baby had been buried on her property. Clyde and his handler came along and checked all around the house, but the bloodhound did not pick up David's scent. The deputy was amazed to find the mother of our accused killer so unhelpful. "How do you *know* Richard did these things?" she kept demanding. Schneider would list the facts—the murder weapon and a victim's wallet were found on him. Still, she didn't seem convinced.

Maps were found in Chase's apartment, and when they reached Schneider he noticed several marks and circles in Lassen County, *one hundred miles north of Sacramento,* tucked on the far eastern boundary of California. Just on the other side of the Nevada border—twenty miles away—was Pyramid Lake.

Schneider knew about Chase's earlier trip to that region, and the deputy wondered if the killer had returned to that desolate area to bury a body. It was surely outside our one-mile circle, but Schneider thought it was worth a look-see. He asked for and received permission to drive to Lassen County.

Up north he could make little sense of the markings on the map. These were large areas, each of them, much too big to search by foot. He checked in with the local sheriff's office, as well as the Highway Patrol and

U.S. Forest Service. Had they stopped this Ranchero or talked to this man? Everywhere he went he showed pictures of Chase and the Ranchero, without a single hit.

He came back bone-tired and a little demoralized, but not about to give up. Once again, as he did almost daily, he called the Ferreiras upon his return and briefed them on his efforts. They were very nice people, he thought, not at all critical or demanding. He knew he would never be able to give them good news—not ever. He just wanted to be able to tell them someday soon, finally and conclusively, what had happened to their baby. And he wanted to bring David home again. Home to be buried.

But was there a body? What exactly *had* Chase done to the baby's body when he took it home? Schneider knew about the bloodstained blender found in Chase's kitchen. The crime lab had determined that animal blood and tissue were present inside it. Had that horrible killer's cocktail come after some concoction involving the baby? Schneider shuddered to think of it. There might not even be a whole body left, just bits and pieces here and there.

Schneider had been a member of the team that had literally dismantled Apartment 15. They took out the traps in the kitchen and bathroom sinks, the tub, and even pulled the toilet off the floor. There were plenty of type A blood samples, but every victim, including the baby—as well as Chase himself—had that blood type. Some tissue was removed and turned over to the crime lab. (It was soon identified as human brain matter.)

Schneider hit me with a new idea one morning.

Suppose he dressed like an inmate and took the cell right next to Chase? "Maybe I can get him to talk to me and tell me about the baby," he said hopefully.

Even though Chase was in the maximum security wing of single-inmate cells, I understood the risks of a cop posing as an inmate, and so did Schneider. Still, I didn't say no but passed his idea on to the higher-ups. Eventually the captain in charge of the jail scotched the idea as far too dangerous.

A double-edged passion drove Schneider on. As a parent of young children he could well imagine the torment Karen and Tony Ferreira must be enduring at the loss and continued absence of their baby. And as a cop Schneider drew a line in the sand when the bad guys started picking on kids. It made him want to go the extra mile.

I received a call from a woman who identified herself as a psychic. She lived in the Bay Area community of Pinole, and she said she could help us. We chatted for a bit, and she seemed very sincere. I passed the note along without comment. I wasn't averse to getting help from any quarter, and neither was Schneider.

He drove out to Pinole and picked up Crystal Finnegan, a fiftyish woman with long gray hair and radiant eyes. On the ride back to Sacramento she explained that she had been in an automobile accident some years back, and when she woke up in the hospital she had this new power.

The psychic stayed in town for a week (we put her up at a downtown hotel), working with Schneider. She went out to the Miroth house and to Chase's apartment, climbed around his Ranchero and the station wagon, all the while holding on to various articles of David's clothing. She could see him, she said, left somewhere where there were "lots of picnic tables."

Schneider checked out several parks in the area, and also school grounds. Again, nothing. The psychic went home disappointed that she didn't break the case for us, and she promised to keep us informed as to any new signals she might be getting from the "other side."

Schneider was getting more desperate by the day. He knew that the longer David's body stayed missing, the less chance there was of ever finding it.

On February 16 Schneider received word from the deputies who worked the county jail.

It seemed Chase was talking.

Wes Garrison, a trustee inmate serving a year of county jail time for repeated drunk driving offenses, reported to his keepers that he had had a discussion the previous day with Richard Chase in which Chase admitted to the killings and provided some new details. Garrison was told he would receive no special treatment for this information, and the trustee agreed, explaining that the offenses for which Chase was in jail so repelled him—"so many murders and the missing baby and all"—that he felt it was the right thing to do.

The conversation was apparently started by Chase, who asked Garrison for a cigarette when the trustee was walking past his cell. As they lit up Chase mumbled a few things about his case, to which Garrison said: "Man, they're charging you with a lot of murders."

Chase said, "Yeah, I know." He then asked Garrison if any of the victims were Germans.

"I don't know," the trustee said.

Chase thought for a moment, then said, "I don't remember how I drank the blood. I just sucked it, I guess."

"Why did you do that?"

"I had to do it," Chase said with conviction. "I have blood poisoning, and I need blood. I was tired of hunting and killing animals so I could drink their blood. I thought about it for several weeks and decided I would kill humans for their blood."

Garrison had never seen Chase in a talkative mood. He spent most of his time on his bunk and seemed to do a lot of sleeping. Usually he kept a pillow over his head. But for some reason the killer wanted to talk that day.

Garrison tried not to show his disgust at what he was hearing. "How did you pick who would be killed?"

"On the first one I was walking down a street near some houses. I was close to a store. I saw a lady out in front of one of the houses. I walked by and watched her. She went into the house, and I followed her. The door was left unlocked. I pulled my gun and went in. As soon as I was inside I saw the lady, and I shot her in the head. She fell to the floor. I took my knife and started to stab and cut her. I then drank some of her blood."

"What about the other murders?" asked the trustee.

"I was walking around just like before. I saw a lady in a house. I walked up to the house. The front door was unlocked. I took my gun out and opened the door and walked in. I came across the lady. She started to scream. I shot her in the head. She fell down. A man came running from another room. He saw me and tried to run away. I shot him in the back of the head. I looked around and saw a boy, just standing there looking."

Chase took a drag off his cigarette.

"This all happened so fast," he went on. "I just shot him, too. I didn't want any witness. Then I heard a baby crying. I went to it. It was screaming and crying. I shot it because it was making so much noise.

"When I heard some knocking at the door I carried the baby out with me. I took it home, where I drank some of its blood. When I was through with it I took the body out and placed it in the garbage."

At the end of the conversation Chase purportedly boasted: "I'm just going to tell them in court that people were driving me insane. That way I will be going to the state hospital and will get out in three years."

". . . took the body out and placed it in the garbage."

But what garbage?

Chase had been arrested on a Saturday, the day after the Miroth killings. Within hours we had searched all the garbage cans and dumpsters not only at the Watt Avenue complex but for blocks around. There had been no city garbage pickup between Friday afternoon and Saturday night or Sunday morning, so if he had disposed of the body in his neighborhood, we would presumably have found it.

Yet the details of Chase's reported jailhouse confession sounded very plausible to us, based on the evidence in the case.

(We turned the complete report of this conversation over to the two deputy district attorneys handling the prosecution, Ronald W. Tochterman and Albert C. Locher. They would decide whether or not to call Wes Garrison to the stand to testify as to his discussion with Chase.)

A weary Schneider was considering another sweep of garbage dumpsters in the East Area, this time with Clyde, when he got a call from an excited citizen who said he'd heard we were looking for a baby's body.

"That's right," the deputy said.

The man gave him directions to the bank of a meandering creek that ran off the American River. "You better get down there fast. There's body parts all over."

Schneider raced to the location.

Indeed, there were body parts scattered about.

Those of a poached deer.

13

Richard Chase had not been an abused child. In fact, he received the love and support of his parents all his life. Still, something went dreadfully wrong.

He was born in 1950, four years before his sister. There was not, as far as anyone could tell, anything very unusual about his childhood, nor did any sibling rivalry develop between the brother and sister. Both his mother and grandmother accused his father of being too strict a disciplinarian and overly critical of his son.

A foreshadowing of what might be did surface in 1960, when Beatrice Chase motioned to a neighbor who lived across the street from them in Sacramento. When the neighbor came over Richard's mother took her to the backyard, where she pointed to some new flower boxes. Mrs. Chase then told her visitor her son, then ten, had buried a cat among the flower boxes.

The neighbor recalled later that quite a few cats were missing from the neighborhood about that time.

During Richard's teen years peace and quiet were the exception at the Chase household, with nonstop parental bickering. The Chases were separated in 1964, and for a short time Richard and his sister Pamela lived with relatives in Los Angeles. But the split hadn't lasted long, and the Chase family soon got back together and returned to the Sacramento area.

For six more years the couple tried to make the marriage work, but they were separated again in 1972 and divorced in 1973.

All that hostile activity, the short separations which eventually became permanent, might have had some effect on the teenager's personality, but it wasn't visible. According to his teenage peers, Richard was popular and had many friends, both male and female. Mira Loma high school classmates of Richard agreed with that assessment of his early teenage behavior. He was, they agreed, neat and well-mannered and well-groomed.

Disregarding outward appearances, Richard might have known better than anyone else that his troubles started when he was a teenager. He dated several girls. Two of these, without having any bad intentions, might have had a profound effect on his life.

Each of the girls was about two years younger than Richard, and each of them considered him their steady date for a while. One young woman tried several times to have sexual intercourse with the boy she called Rick. It was not possible because he could not maintain an erection. Again, with another young

164

woman, Richard attempted intercourse and was unable to function.

As a senior in high school he attended a party where booze was plentiful. Richard recalled he had more than enough to drink that night. He had run down a street after he became drunk, shouting something, or at least making a noise no one could understand. One of his friends chased him down the street, stopped his headlong flight, and took him home, where he sobered up. Richard admitted to his friend at the time that his inability to function sexually affected him deeply. That December, when he was eighteen, he visited a psychiatrist who specialized in adolescent problems. Richard told him about his impotence and admitted he had failed in attempts to have sex with three women.

At the time Richard had been concerned about his emotional stability, and the problems his family was having bothered him deeply. He remembered being told, among other things, that suppressed anger is the most common cause of male impotence. The anger, he learned, was often directed at women in general.

(Richard was not told, for good reason, that some persons can only achieve sexual gratification through acts of sadism that include injuring their partner. Neither had he been told that impotence was often found in the history of sexual psychopaths.)

If he was at all honest with himself, Richard Chase, at twenty-seven years of age, must have known he did not live up to the "nice guy" image he had been tagged with as a teenager. As he progressed through high school his school records and history reflected a growing defiance of authority that grew into open rebellion before his years at Mira Loma ended with his graduation. There were times—and they became more frequent as he grew older—when he was hopelessly selfish and inconsiderate. He told false stories when convenient—when the truth would not help him.

He rationalized his actions and, as often as not, blamed his misfortune and bad luck on other people. He was quick with alibis or explanations when he strayed from the truth or from what is normally regarded as acceptable behavior.

Arrested for possession of marijuana when he was about sixteen years old, rather than being ashamed of his own behavior he was outraged at his father for refusing to hire a lawyer to defend him.

Later the elder Chase suspected he was still using the illegal weed, and Richard remembered flushing a bag of the stuff down the toilet to avoid being caught.

A year later, when he was a high school senior, Richard was caught stealing a bottle of liquor from a neighbor. He showed no embarrassment or remorse concerning the theft. (Lack of conscience is the undeniable mark of a psychopath.)

As his behavior deteriorated, so did Richard's grades. He managed to graduate from high school by the skin of his teeth. He thought about college and was encouraged to continue his education by his family. For a couple of years he bounced in and out of a junior college. His grades were less than average, and the elder Chase noticed that fewer and fewer of his son's old friends visited him at his home. Richard's appearance deteriorated. His hair grew, and he was somewhat scroungy. His mother didn't, or wouldn't, notice the difference. She told her friends her son didn't look any different from other youths who were members of his generation. (It *was* the era of hippies.)

When he was just twenty years old, in 1970, Richard moved out of what he must have viewed as the restrictive atmosphere of his parents' home and into a house on Annadale Lane. He had two roommates, both of them young women. One of them he had known in high school; the other was a friend she had met since graduation.

There was no love lost between him and his roommates in the house on Annadale Lane. The older of the two girls described Richard as a slob, complaining that he seldom if ever bathed and never washed his clothes. To her mind his behavior was generally repulsive. More and more he seemed to withdraw from his surroundings and from the things and people he had known. Visits from his friends were few and eventually became virtually nonexistent. As far as his roommates could tell, Richard Chase did not have *any* friends.

The time came when, alone in the house, he boarded closed the door to his bedroom and knocked a hole in the wall of his closet. He then nailed shut his closet door from the inside. Asked to explain his weird behavior, he told people he had to nail the door shut. People had been sneaking up on him from the inside.

Richard's strange behavior scared his roommates, and they asked him to move. He refused, and, not wanting to pursue an argument with "a crazy," they moved out.

According to his former roommates, Richard was

using marijuana on a daily basis before they left. Nor, according to them, did he restrict himself to marijuana. They said he was a user of any and all drugs that came his way, including barbiturates and amphetamines.

Once, the roommates said, Richard walked out of his room entirely naked, sat down, and opened an unintelligible conversation with some girls who were visiting his roommates.

Another time during his residence at the Annadale house a friend of his attended a party there and claimed that as the evening wore on he found Richard lying on the floor moaning and making strange noises. At the moment, the visitor said, Chase did not seem able to talk in any intelligible way.

One female guest at an Annadale party remembered Chase leaning out of a window and waving a gun at someone on the street.

In 1973 a young lady was visiting the apartment of a young man whom she would later marry. Her boyfriend was there, as was one of his friends. Sometime that evening Chase visited the apartment. He was drinking from a bottle wrapped in a paper bag. For a short time she was left alone in the apartment with Chase while the other two men went to buy more beer. While they were gone Richard began "touching and grabbing" at the woman and wouldn't stop even after she insisted he quit. He followed her around the room, making no bones about his lecherous intent. She was very frightened by his behavior.

The men returned, and she reported Chase's antics. They ordered him to leave, but instead of doing so Richard had a fit. He delivered a screaming falsetto oration declaring that no one had a right to tell him what to do or when to leave. An hour of arguing followed before Richard finally left. He returned a short time later, saying he had left his cigarettes.

Once in the house again Richard began shouting and pushing one of the men, saying no one could make him do anything he didn't want to do. A fight broke out.

During the brawl a small handgun fell out of Richard's pocket. The second young man grabbed the gun and threw it into the bedroom. Richard was still shouting, telling the world at large no one could tell him what to do and go ahead and call the police, he didn't care if the police were called. Eventually the deputies came, and he was taken away to something less than comfortable lodgings in the county jail.

Richard's life began sliding steadily downhill. He did not work often and had trouble holding jobs. If he was in serious trouble, he was seldom caught, and then for only minor infractions. But his behavior was often strange to the point of being irrational, and even his friends—the few he had—considered him weird.

His search for his place in the world took him to Utah in 1972. There he was arrested for a minor traffic violation just serious enough to demand bail money. His father put up bail. When he returned to California he complained to both parents he had been gassed while in jail. His physical appearance had deteriorated, and he complained constantly about unusual (and even impossible) injuries and ailments. He told anyone who would listen his stomach was turned around and "backwards" and that his heart frequently stopped beating.

During this period Chase's parents separated, and they eventually divorced.

Chase lived with his father for a while in 1973, complaining all the while that he was nervous and that he had a rapid pulse. His father took him to a hospital, and Richard was diagnosed as having hypertension; medication was prescribed for him. About then the elder Chase started some do-it-yourself home improvement projects. Richard decided to help. He began by assisting his father, who was laying a new floor in the kitchen and had several fledgling projects. Sometimes Richard worked alone and unsupervised. His work was perfectly acceptable. But when his father suggested he go out and get a job Richard replied that he was still sick and had to build up his strength before he tried working for an employer outside the family.

During this time Chase missed owning a car and complained constantly about not having one. Some arguments ensued about whether Richard should own a car when he was not strong enough to hold a regular job. The arguments with his father continued, and Richard finally moved back in with his mother.

Chase could not have been eating well. He was bone-thin when he rejoined his mother. His sister thought he was about as skinny as a man could get. She also thought that her brother had become "spooky." More than once she ran from the house, terrorized by his violent temper tantrums.

Unable to get along with either parent, Richard lived for a while with his grandmother. That involved a trip to Los Angeles and helping his grandmother, who, with Richard's uncle, helped operate a school for the developmentally disabled. For a while Richard drove a bus transporting the students to and from school.

He didn't make things easy for himself. Nervous and upset most of the time, he complained constantly about heart and stomach discomfort.

His relatives were not exactly happy with his behavior. Richard was not a pleasing spectacle. He flatly refused to keep his clothes or his hands clean. Sometimes he was guilty of angry, hostile, and peculiar behavior. There was nothing rational about some of the things he did. (Normal people, for example, didn't nail shut closet doors as a mean of protection.)

Returning to Sacramento and his mother's home in the mid-seventies, Richard went to several physicians for examination. Once he decided he had cardiac arrest and called the fire department. Fire trucks and an ambulance arrived at the Chase home, but the paramedic who arrived with the rest of the equipment refused to treat the patient. Whatever his reason, he suggested to Richard's mother that she take him to a hospital. She accepted his advice, and Richard was admitted to the American River Hospital. The date was December 1, 1973. Richard was at his best or his worst, depending on the point of view. He told the attending physician his heart and kidneys had stopped working, his stomach hurt, his pulmonary artery had been stolen, and his blood had stopped flowing. The physician could find nothing medically wrong with the patient.

A psychiatrist talked with Richard in the emergency

room. He noted that the patient was filthy and foul-smelling. The doctor would note he found him a "wild-eyed" man who appeared to suffer from delusions.

Richard followed his regular practice by complaining long and loud. He said his entire body was numb, particularly the chest. At the same time he indicated he felt pains in the chest, and that discomfort he was experiencing in other parts of his body suggested he might also be suffering from a hernia.

It was possible, he told the doctor, that he was suffering from an aneurysm, adding it might be best if he was put in an intensive care unit. Richard defended his sanity. He flatly and emphatically denied hearing voices or that he was afflicted with auditory hallucinations of any kind. He told the doctors he had read articles about the heart, lungs, and stomach of human beings, implying he knew as much about the subject of medicine as did any of his attending physicians.

One of the psychiatrists who examined him came up with a strongly negative report. He had the impression that the patient was suffering a schizophrenic reaction to his symptoms and trying to interpret mild complaints on his own.

The doctor's diagnosis indicated Richard was suffering from chronic paranoid schizophrenic condition. Regardless, he believed a toxic psychosis resulting from the use of drugs could not be ruled out. He ordered Richard to be held in the psychiatric ward for seventy-two hours of observation.

Because the doctor felt Richard was not a danger to himself or anyone else, he was not held under close confinement. Richard was allowed to leave the hospital without permission, which he soon did. The first time his mother returned him to the hospital. The second time she told the doctors that her son had said someone was bothering him at the hospital, and she had decided to handle the problem at home. That would be necessary because the psychiatrist in charge of Richard's case refused to treat him except in the hospital. He told Beatrice that while he felt Richard needed treatment and care, he was not a danger to himself or anyone else.

Discharged from the hospital in December, 1973, Richard immediately began complaining about physical disabilities again. Taken by his mother to another doctor, Chase told the physician he had a heart condition and vascular disability, the result of head and back injuries. He also admitted to the doctor that he had been using LSD and marijuana, although not recently.

Unable to find anything physically wrong with Richard, the doctor ordered a brain scan, electrocardiogram, and thyroid tests. None of them showed any physical abnormalities. Three days later Chase told his new doctor his heart had stopped and asked for papers that would admit him to the intensive care unit of the hospital. Again his physician found nothing wrong, and he ordered tranquilizers.

Three years later, in 1976, Richard visited the same physician in January and February. He was, Chase explained, applying for Social Security assistance and welfare because he could not work. The doctor examined him, found a generally weakened condition, and recommended him for welfare because his rundown condition had made him an impossible job candidate. Richard was coherent and well behaved throughout the meetings, though the doctor said his patient seemed to be neurotic.

Another physician who specialized in neurology had some comments to make about Chase's physical appearance. He observed his new patient was at best unkempt-looking. Portions of Richard's hair had been shaved almost to the scalp. He complained, as usual, about a variety of difficulties. One of these was swelling in the back of his head. Richard asked for a spinal tap and an angiogram. He told the doctor he was dieting and felt he could cure himself that way. The doctor, a specialist, found nothing neurologically wrong. He did, in response to Chase's repeated complaints, have X-rays taken of his patient's skull, with negative results.

Again the doctor decided Chase's judgment was not impaired in any way. His patient had a satisfactory memory, was coherent, and knew what he was doing. He did not claim to be hearing voices or claim anyone was controlling his thoughts. His memory was all right, and he spoke coherently.

Five months after leaving the hospital Richard Chase was exercising and had gained weight. Then he appeared to slip away from the real world. He accused his mother of poisoning him and threw his meals on the floor when she prepared them. He had started cooking for himself and would not drink from an open milk carton. Once he thought the milk tasted funny. Both Richard's mother and his sister tried it and thought it smelled and tasted like dishwashing soap. His sister believed Richard had actually flavored the milk with the soap.

Richard was relentless. He convinced his mother she should buy an oxygen tent after he read an article that told him heart patients used them.

Through the mid-seventies his mother was convinced he held conversations with an imaginary person, believing his fictional friend was sending him messages by mental telepathy. Twice he accused his mother of controlling his mind. His sister heard one of the accusations. She did not remember anything about him hearing voices.

His father demanded that he move from his mother's house. He let Richard stay with him for a while with a clear understanding that he must move as soon as he found a place to live. The two of them located an apartment for Richard on Cannon Street, which he moved into for about six weeks. His rent was paid by his father. The elder Chase tried to do his best in a bad situation. He paid Richard's rent and visited him once or twice a week, delivering groceries during those visits.

During that period Richard began riding his bicycle to a nearby rabbit farm. He bought rabbits there and butchered them at home. He did not complain about physical ailments or any other problems. His father, who did not know about the rabbits, thought his son was doing well.

Abruptly, Richard took a turn for the worse. On an April evening in 1976 he was found by his father, sitting in his apartment with his door open, pale and sick, wearing only his shorts. Chase told his father he had purchased a bad rabbit and thought he had food poisoning. He was promptly taken to the hospital and admitted to the emergency room at Sacramento Community. The physician on call observed the patient was emaciated, pale, dirty, and in a state of shock. His vital signs indicated he might be sick. Examination revealed he had blood poisoning. At first the physician who treated him believed he could have had some kind of a septic shock, although he did not expect that kind of blood poisoning as the result of eating animal blood or parts. Dirty needles, the physician reflected, would be a more likely cause of the illness, although he didn't see the telltale tracks normally found on a heavy narcotics user's arms.

Chase was completely irrational, the doctor thought. Chase wanted to be moved because he was afraid of contracting a disease from one of the other patients in the ward. His trouble, Richard explained, was caused by having eaten a rabbit that had eaten battery acid that had seeped through the walls of his stomach and into his flesh. His blood pressure, the patient insisted, was zero. Tests taken by the doctors revealed no abnormality in the size or shape of Richard's heart or, as might be suspected, any disease of the patient's lungs.

When he consulted the patient's parents the doctor was told Richard had a history of drug abuse, including marijuana, LSD, and narcotics.

Chase's behavior convinced the doctor he was suffering from paranoid schizophrenia, and he was transferred to the psychiatric unit at American River Hospital. There the doctors agreed Chase did suffer from "somatic delusions," claiming his body was falling apart and his circulatory system was not functioning. His father was finding his son belligerent, destructive, uncontrollable.

On April 28, 1976, Chase was again admitted to American River. His doctor ordered a fourteen-day hold for further psychiatric study on the patient and on May 3, 1976 started conservatorship proceedings. Richard was put on a waiting list for transfer to Beverly Manor, a skilled nursing facility for mental patients.

Richard Narver of the Sacramento Public Guardian's Office also recommended a conservatorship for Richard after interviewing him on May 16. During his interview Chase was agitated, suspicious, and guarded. He reported that he drank rabbit blood because of his weak heart. But he did not contest the conservatorship proceedings, and when the hearings were over he went right back to square one. His parents were appointed his conservators. The conservatorship began June 2, 1976 and would automatically end a year later unless someone wanted it to be renewed.

The doctors, by the way, did indicate that the failure of antipsychotic drugs to affect Richard supported the theory that his was a toxic psychosis. In other words, some outside agent, such as narcotics, could have caused it. Someone who took drugs such as LSD could be mistaken for a schizophrenic, and Thorazine, a drug that had been taken by Richard, could cause a person to mimic the symptoms of schizophrenia.

Richard was coherent enough to announce he had spoken to a lawyer and to ask what would happen if he left the hospital. Told he would be returned to either the hospital staff or the sheriff, he replied that he did not want that to happen.

Although he was aware of the probable results, Richard ran away from the hospital two days later. The escape was not difficult. He simply ran out the door and when captured struggled desperately. Richard managed to break free. The next day his father returned him to the hospital, and he was transferred to Beverly Manor, the facility specializing in the treatment of mental patients.

At Beverly Manor Richard earned a nickname, which was given to him by his fellow patients.

That nickname was "Dracula."

Not surprising, since throughout his stay at the institution he revealed a preoccupation with blood. When he talked at all, it was inevitably about killing animals. Once he announced to everyone listening that it was easy to kill and butcher rabbits because they looked like mechanical toys.

One day Chase was found with fresh blood on his face. Two dead birds, their necks broken, were found just outside the window of his room.

His parents, as conservators, had the authority to remove him from Beverly Manor. His mother decided he should be somewhere else. When she made that decision she and her husband had Richard discharged. He checked out of Beverly Manor September 29, 1976. His doctor believed he had developed "good socialization" and had a "realistic view" of his problems. His discharge summary stated his thinking was clearer than when he had entered the establishment.

Richard rented an apartment (#12) at the Watt

Avenue complex at that time. (Another point that fit our psychological profile: our killer had been recently discharged from a mental hospital.) He received $246 a month in Social Security. His mother usually cashed the check and used it to pay for rent and utilities. She shopped for his groceries and was pleased when her son did not act strange or complain about physical problems.

About that time, Richard's parents were notified that it was time to make up their minds whether or not to renew the conservatorship. They decided they should not, and it ended June 2, 1977.

For a while Richard lived up to his obligations. He kept appointments with his physician in October and December but failed to show up for a third date. He began to have new physical problems. He told his doctor he had headaches and believed they were caused by a blood clot in his head. The doctor performed a computerized brain scan that revealed nothing wrong.

Shortly after the conservatorship ended in 1977 Richard moved out of his apartment and left for Washington, D.C. He traveled by himself, carrying $1,000 in retroactive Social Security payments. After an eighteen-day absence he returned with one extra possession: the Ford Ranchero, which he had bought in Colorado.

Richard stayed with his mother a few days, then moved back into the Watt Avenue building, this time into Apartment 15.

A touch—perhaps more than a touch—of sadism had been demonstrated by Richard that summer. His mother confessed later she had seen him abuse the German shepherd, and that he appeared to enjoy watching it suffer.

Beatrice Chase had finally had enough, and she declined to invite him over for Christmas dinner. Every time he came to her house he would start trouble. He was such a difficult boy—even as a youngster he would never fess up to having done anything wrong. And his answers, when he was pressed, would as often as not be nonsensical. A simple query like "When are you going to get a haircut?" would be answered with: "What did you say your middle name is?"

She relented some on Christmas, taking him something to eat. They exchanged a few presents at his front door. He refused to let her inside his apartment anymore because she always complained about it being so dirty and smelly. Richard had refused her repeated offers to clean the place up for him.

Richard's father had been involved with his son over the Christmas holidays, too. He even let Richard choose his own Christmas present.

Richard picked out an orange ski parka.

Four days after Christmas Ambrose Griffin died.

The Griffin shooting was a confidence-builder for Richard Chase, who was ready to graduate from dogs and other animals. He had practiced and was a good enough shot to have hit the man the first time, but he missed. He was so excited he'd pulled the gun off its target with the first shot. He squeezed off a second shot rapidly, putting it right in the chest of the middle-aged man standing on the lawn. He must have been sure as he accelerated past the house on Robertson Avenue that the man was dead or dying.

It had been so easy that Richard Chase got to thinking he could get away with killing people.

On the morning of January 21, 1978 Richard and his father went rock hunting together. Both enjoyed themselves, and the older man observed his son did not complain about any physical ailments. That was a good sign.

The elder Chase saw his son again a couple of days later. He was acting nervous and impatient this time but said nothing out of the ordinary. His speech was perfectly coherent and his conversation reasonable.

His father offered to buy him groceries, but Richard said he didn't need any. The son readily agreed with his father's suggestion that they take another rock-hunting trip soon. Yes, it *had* been fun.

That second visit ended shortly after ten o'clock on the morning of January 23, 1978.

Within hours Teresa Wallin would be dead.

14

March 24, 1978

Oscar Rossow, a janitor for Arcade Wesleyan Church near the corner of Whitney and Watt avenues, noticed an outside gate behind the church was ajar. That was unusual because the gate was always kept locked, thereby keeping out of sight an area that contained a variety of junk, some of which would be kept and some thrown out.

When he went to lock the gate the janitor noticed a cardboard box lying on its side, threatening to spill its contents. He went to right it and then caught the odor. Something dead was inside, Rossow realized.

A dog?

A cat?

Oh my God, no he thought. A human baby!

Detective Fred Homen answered the call to Homicide, listened for a moment or so, and motioned to me to pick up the phone. I listened while the church pastor, Reverend Robert D. Hughes, reported the janitor's find.

I asked the preacher to keep people out of the area, then I called Dispatch and had them send out patrol units to seal the area pronto. I realized immediately that the scene was less than a mile from Chase's apartment.

Having a gut feeling about what we would find, I put in a call to Bill Schneider, who, much to his chagrin, had run out of leads and places to search about a week or ten days before and had gone back to his assignment with Special Enforcement Detail.

The reverend, shaken and upset, greeted us in the church parking lot and pointed to the fenced gate at the rear of the church. I was pleased to see that several patrol units had already sealed off the area, keeping bystanders back a safe distance.

A paved pathway led from the "junk" enclosure to the rear of a market that was located behind the church. The path appeared to be little used and seldom visited.

"The janitor was investigating an open gate," the pastor explained as we walked in that direction. "Like I said, he found a body that looks like a little boy."

A little boy.

I thought about Karen and Tony Ferreira.

I wanted to turn around and walk away. Go anywhere, do anything else, let someone finish the job here. But to have done so would have been unconscionable.

The cardboard box was still lying on its side.

I went to the box and peered inside.

There was the body, or at least part of the body, of a

small child in the box. It had been decapitated, and there was no sign of its head. The small corpse was partially mummified, no doubt from being protected and preserved somewhat by the container. Even so, it was decaying, and a stench—the sweet, sickly odor of rotting human flesh—emanated from the box.

A pair of red corduroy trousers was sitting in front of the top of the open box. A patch on the back of the pants read "Sesame Street."

Schneider arrived about the same time as Dr. Pierce Rooney, pathologist, and James Hosang, supervising deputy of the coroner's office. The three of them went to the box.

I had observed the arrival of TV news crews and thought they were shooting from behind the barricade. But I now realized that some of them had gotten on the roof of the building adjacent to the church and were shooting down on the area that held the box and its contents.

At the same time the pathologist was trying to get a better look at the body.

I was determined to keep the TV crews from getting the shot they so badly wanted. Little David Ferreira's mummified body was *not* going to be "film at eleven."

Someone found a sheet in one of the vans, and we spread it out, holding it above the box, thereby blocking the media's bird's-eye view.

The criminalist noticed that the box was sealed on the bottom with gray duct tape. He recalled that there had been a roll of similar tape in Chase's apartment.

They now opened the box completely.

The corpse was lying on its back, right arm draped across the stomach, left arm extended. We were able to see from our new vantage point that the child's arms and legs had not been amputated, as some of us originally thought, but were simply hidden by the body. The severed baby's head, we could now see, was lying under the torso. What seemed to be gunpowder tattooing scarred the side of the child's head. It centered on a hole in the side of the head that appeared to have been made by a small-caliber weapon.

A green, red, and brown sweater was lying between the child's legs, and he still wore light blue diaper-type underpants. The little boy was blond.

"That's the clothes David was wearing," Schneider offered. He stood up, arms akimbo, as if suddenly viewing the scene from afar. "It's him."

Schneider followed the coroner's wagon to the morgue and was there less than an hour later when they laid the body out, preparing it for autopsy.

When the last of the cardboard was removed and someone started cutting away at the rotted fabric of the boy's clothes, a metallic sound was heard.

The pathologist reached under one of the boy's legs and produced a ring of keys.

Schneider had no doubt one was a car key. He even had a good idea what car it would fit, and he was right.

A certain red station wagon in our impound lot.

After the procedure Schneider hurriedly went to see the Ferreiras. He wanted to be the one to tell them.

When he did, Karen said over and over, trying to be strong but on the verge of tears: "Are you *sure?*"

On the surface she had accepted for some time that her baby was dead, but hidden inside had been one glimmer of hope that was now so difficult to extinguish. She still dreamed at night that she was rocking her baby, only to awaken to his empty nursery, which she had left unchanged.

"Are you *sure?*" she asked again.

Each time he was asked the question Bill Schneider said softly, so very sadly, "Yes. I'm sorry."

15

Legal proceedings were still months away when the trial watch began.

A new personality had entered the case of The People of the State of California versus Richard Trenton Chase. The lead prosecutor, Ronald W. Tochterman, Assistant Chief Deputy District Attorney, was a real veteran. He was head of the county's major crimes unit, and all murder cases landed on his desk. Though he assigned a number of them to his subordinates, he kept a good many for himself. Like most outstanding prosecutors, he greatly preferred trial work to administrative labors that kept him out of court.

Tochertman, tall and reed-thin, had a reputation for being an intellectual, and beyond that, for making himself an expert in whatever arena a case landed in. I had seen him do it before, and it was truly an amazing transformation. To describe him as a hard worker would be a disservice. Intense and extremely focused, he possessed work habits that paralleled those of a well-engineered machine that could run twenty-four hours a day without overheating.

There was not any question in Tochterman's mind that Richard Chase was the East Area Killer, nor did he have much doubt that Chase would be convicted of killing six people. He suspected early on that the opposition would launch an insanity defense. That would be the crux of the case, Tochterman knew, and would decide whether or not Chase answered for his crimes or received sanctuary in a state mental hospital.

Tochterman was firmly intent on making sure that the prisoner pay for his murderous acts to the fullest extent prescribed by law. He thought of the defendant in terms of his being a danger to society and was determined that, if at all possible, Chase be put in a position where he could never kill again. There was only one way to do that. The D.A. intended to ask for the death penalty.

There was no doubt in the minds of the prosecuting team—which included Al Locher, a young deputy D.A., and experienced investigator Dixon Davey— that Chase would add the plea of not guilty by reason of insanity to his original plea of innocence. (He soon did.) One way or another, Chase had to prove diminished capacity or face an inevitable death sentence.

To Tochterman went the task of proving that Chase was legally sane. That, people might believe, was an impossible task. But they did not take into consideration three factors, the first two being human components. One was the skill and talent of the lead prosecutor. The second was the psychological makeup of Richard Chase himself. And third was the law itself regarding the thorny issue of sanity as applied to criminal responsibility.

The task assigned to Tochterman was tough, but not impossible. He had to prove that Chase, at the time the murders were committed, was able to "appreciate the criminality of his actions and was able to conform his conduct to the confines of the law." In a nutshell: did Chase know the difference between right and wrong, and could he have made a choice not to commit murder? That was the legal fence that protected Chase from the finality of California's death penalty. If the prosecutor could convince the jury that Chase had killed (easy), knew it was *wrong to kill* (not easy), and *had a choice* (not easy), he would be convicted and quite possibly sent to the gas chamber.

To prove sanity was never easy. It is always difficult to try to climb into another person's mind, particularly a person as warped as Richard Chase.

But Tochterman would try.

I visited the prosecutor in his office one day. He was behind his desk, submerged in a sea of legal tomes. He was furiously typing with his left hand on an old manual typewriter he had used since his college days. With his right hand he scrawled notes on a legal pad. At the same time he looked up at me through his round-rimmed spectacles and queried me smartly on several points concerning the case. As far as I could tell, his mind was headed down three diverse paths at once without getting lost.

Tochterman took a week's vacation to catch up on his legal reading. In the mountain cabin he rented he found a hardcover book that scrutinized the legend of Dracula. A scholarly work, it was written by a professor at San Francisco State. Tochterman read it from cover to cover in two days and fired off a memo to Al Locher on things for him to do. (The memo was one and a half pages long, typed, single-spaced—this from a man on vacation.)

Tochterman immersed himself in the history of blood and blood-related crimes. Blood, he learned, had been used in medicine back to the days of primitive man, spanning continents and oceans without discrimination. Native Australians commonly gave human blood to the sick and old, believing it would strengthen them. It was not, however, always necessary for the infirm patient to drink the blood. Often it was satisfactory when blood was sprinkled on the body of the sufferer.

An old German poem told of Burgundians who, when besieged in their burning halls by the invading Huns, drank the blood of their fallen comrades in the hope they could maintain their strength.

There were beliefs of the followers of several primitive religions that blood was life. It followed naturally for some primitive people that a person could add to his own life by drinking blood, rubbing himself with it, or using it during sacred rites and rituals.

Tochterman's homework revealed that during the 1890s ladies went to a Paris slaughterhouse to swallow a medicinal glass of blood. Four hundred years earlier the blood of three teenage boys was reported to have been given to Pope Innocent VII during an attempt (unsuccessful) to rejuvenate him.

The prosecutor became an expert, too, on the motives in ritualistic killings and the psychological makeup of people who ingested the blood of their victims. He learned that members of many primitive tribes drank the blood of their enemies to enhance their own strength. External application was favored by others. The various rites of blood brotherhood reached into some present-day ceremonies. Native Australians, before setting out on a revenge mission, would drink blood. They also had some sprinkled on their bodies.

He also learned that isolated individuals who claimed therapeutic justification in their appetite for blood often rationalized the true motives for their killing. These could include sexual sadism combined with a perverse desire to kill, mutilate, and drink blood. Such tendencies included an "aberration of erotic blood lust known as haemostodipsia."

Theory held that such people desire blood not only during the act of coitus but at other times. They get their sexual satisfaction through their teeth and mouth. What coitus is to the lover, the bite and sucking of blood is to the haemotodipsiac. The fixation, some researchers believed, is often tied up with necrophilia.

There are people, some researchers believe, who experience sexual pathology and a sensual joy at the sight of flowing blood.

Tochterman and his staff absorbed as much information about these sects and those who ingested either human or animal blood as they had time for. The prosecutor knew that when he went to trial, he would face a lineup of psychiatrists—some who would agree with the prosecution and others who wouldn't.

If he was going to succeed in making Chase pay the ultimate price for his crimes, Tochterman would have to be able to "outshrink" the shrinks.

In June, 1978 the court appointed two psychiatrists to examine Richard Chase and report as to his competency to stand trial. Neither of these doctors would delve into the complex sanity issue. Rather, they were commissioned simply to determine whether or not Chase, in their professional judgment, understood the charges against him and would be able to assist in his defense. Separately, they interviewed Chase in jail and found him competent to go on trial for murder. Now the legal proceedings began in earnest.

Predictably, the defense quickly petitioned for a change in venue. One survey found that the name Richard Chase had a ninety-five percent recognition factor in Sacramento County, with most of the respondents believing him guilty. Understandably, the court granted the venue change, and the trial was moved 120 miles to the south, where Santa Clara County Superior Court Judge John Schatz (newly elected from the municipal court) became the presiding judge.

Psychiatric testimony would prove vital to both sides during the guilt and penalty phase, and by the time it was over a dozen psychiatrists would have examined the defendant, with many being called to testify.

The opinions of two psychiatrists brought in by the prosecution proved pivotal.

Dr. Martin Beimer of Fresno, California interviewed Chase four times for a total of four and a half hours.

Chase began by denying any knowledge of the murders he was accused of committing and went on to complain about the food in jail, asking the psychiatrist to take "evidence" to court with him that would prove his jailers, or someone, were trying to poison him.

The doctor also listened to Richard's account of several unsuccessful encounters with women and his continuing impotence.

Chase again maintained he did not really know he had killed anyone and had no memory of the actual killings. As the interviews progressed, however, the prisoner told Dr. Beimer he "sort of remembered the crimes," the crimes for which he was charged.

Typical of his early remarks to Dr. Beimer: "It could have been someone else. I don't remember who they were because I was sick, poisoned by iodine or mercury. I can't stand it. I can't get away from it."

Chase interrupted his account to mention that he had been sick and couldn't hold a job. Then, prompted by the physician, he went back to the murders. He rambled on that the murders had happened over a "couple of weeks" and that "knives and guns" were used.

He progressed to: "I don't really remember anything about it. I was trying to get free of poison and go

193

live with my grandmother's relatives. The car had broken down, and I had no money, so I walked into someone's house and killed them. A lot of people in that neighborhood had been poisoning me for years, and now it's spread to the jail."

By the end of the second interview he flat-out told Dr. Beimer, "I killed somebody and got caught afterwards. I don't know much about it. I've gotten involved with the Italians, who are after me because I killed some of them. I killed about six of them. It happened over a weekend or a week." He mentioned "little pieces of strychnine" to the doctor and said he killed because he was suffering. "I couldn't stand it, so I went crazy and then to jail."

Dr. Beimer waited until the third interview before asking Chase about the animals.

It turned out that if Richard Chase was sorry for anything he'd done, his grief centered around the animals he had killed. He seemed genuinely sorry, and even remembered that he had killed a cat named Calico Kitten in 1973 or 1974. He had picked up the kitten, he told the doctor, at his girlfriend's house when he was a senior in high school. He raised the cat, he said, and then when he was watching a television he saw a program that showed a cat getting good medical treatment.

"I couldn't get good medical treatment from either doctors or hospitals," Richard complained.

He went on to describe taking the cat out to the rear of the house, killing it, and drinking some of its blood, hoping the treatment would help his weakness. He went through the process with other animals, including a white dog named Sabbath, then rabbits and some birds.

Asked if he thought drinking the blood had helped his medical condition, Chase sadly admitted it had not.

Richard recalled putting a cup by the bullet holes in the animals so he could catch the blood and drink it.

For no apparent reason he offered that he had seen an angiogram performed on educational television and that it fascinated him to watch a heart pumping blood.

Asked if he would have killed people if a policeman had been standing by, Chase replied, "I don't know."

Richard denied that he had an urge to drink human blood. He told the doctor he just thought it would be "therapeutic."

He expressed some remorse, saying he did not feel right about the people he killed. "It was not fair to kill those people. I could have tried medical places out of town, but I went to a lot of places and couldn't find any help." He admitted having nightmares about the people he killed, and he worried that they might "come back from the dead," but he said that he had not seen or heard from them.

All of Chase's self-claimed delusions did not help him in critical ways with the psychiatrist.

To the court, Dr. Beimer wrote:

My opinion is that Richard Chase is seeking relief from intolerable distress associated with his belief that he was being poisoned to death, and that his belief was due to a severe chronic mental disorder. He believed that drinking blood was a possible solution to save him from certain death. [But] *he understood that he was killing people and that it was wrong to kill people.*

The italicized words would later prove critical to Chase's insanity defense. Despite his professed delusions about drinking blood for whatever reason, he knew he was wrong to kill his victims.

Dr. Leland Silva, a Sacramento psychiatrist, interviewed the defendant five times for a total of four hours.

He had less success in getting Chase to talk about the murders. In fact, the accused repeatedly stated that he didn't remember any killings, though once, after the doctor had put his notepad and pencil away, he offered: "I didn't kill anybody. I didn't kill anybody, just a few people. Anyway, I didn't kill all those people like they said I did. I just killed a few people. Well, I think it was a family over behind Country Club."

In conclusion, Dr. Silva found Chase to be a "paranoid, antisocial personality" but "not schizophrenic."

The cardinal finding of schizophrenia, namely the involuntary and uncontrollable disruption of the normal flow of thought processes, is nowhere evident in this case. . . . [There was a] distinct shift in his manner as we approached discussion of the sensitive areas. He consistently became cautious, withdrawn, evasive and refused to discuss matters. He has a well-developed sense of right and wrong.

At various points it was my clear impression that he was intentionally evading the question . . . seeking to present the picture of an individual suffering from a serious psychiatric disorder; however, upon further specific questioning I obtained no evidence of psychiatric disorder other than his delusional system.

The two psychiatrists found Chase sane.

On January 2, 1979, more than a full year after Richard Trenton Chase fired the shot that killed Ambrose Griffin, his trial on six counts of murder began.

The underpinning of Ron Tochterman's case rested on these words from one of the court-appointed psychiatrists: "[Chase] was capable of not killing people. *He had that choice.*"

Time and again Tochterman supported that premise during his evidentiary presentation in his case.

He had that choice.

Tochterman had assigned to his assistant, Al Locher, the job of keeping track of all the evidence in the case, amounting to 250 prosecution exhibits. Locher also handled the direct testimony of those government witnesses who took the stand to testify about the physical evidence collected at the crime scenes. When it was over Locher would describe his experience working beside Tochterman as "a clinic in how to try a murder case. . . . Ron only knew one way to play the game: full-press. There was no hiding the ball. He believed in just overwhelming the opposition."

The first witness called to the stand was David Wallin, who recounted finding his wife's mutilated body. In all, nearly a hundred witnesses testified for the prosecution. They included the widow, Carol Griffin; the schoolmate, Nancy Holden; the mother, Karen Ferreira; the best friend, Neone Grangaard; the next-door neighbor, Dawn Larson; the pathologists, Dr. Joseph Masters and Dr. Pierce Rooney; the criminalist, Alan Gilmore; and from the Sheriff's Department, Detectives Don Habecker, Fred Homen, Wayne Irey, Bill Roberts, and yours truly. (I testified as to what I observed at both the Wallin and Miroth crime scenes.)

A roomful of evidence was introduced at the trial, and most of it pointed clearly to Chase as the East Area Killer. The wallet belonging to Daniel Meredith was enough to tie him to the Merrywood address of Evelyn Miroth. And of course, there was the .22 he was carrying in his coveted shoulder holster when he was arrested—the gun that had killed them all.

One troublesome circumstance we had been confronted with in the investigation, which followed us all the way to court—the fact that Chase and every one of his victims had the same blood type—would not be a problem today, when blood types can be broken down into enzymes. The odds of six blood types from six different people being the same would be nothing short of astronomical.

Actually, the similarity of blood types turned out to be academic. Richard Chase had convicted himself, to a large measure, by having carried the sufficiently damning evidence on his person at the time of his arrest. The .22 and the wallet would have done the job themselves.

It surprised us all when Chase took the stand in his own defense. Possibly his lawyer hoped to rack up points for his insanity defense by revealing his client to be something less than mentally balanced. And possibly Chase himself believed the jury would sympathize with him because he had been "mistreated" by so many people throughout his young life.

Chase did not attempt to deny the murders, though he claimed a foggy memory concerning some of the details.

In mounting a rambling confession from the witness stand the defense was willing to lose the guilt phase of the trial in the hope of winning what would be the second phase: the jury's determination of Chase's sanity.

As Chase gave his version of the Griffin killing and some of the events that happened in his life around that time he seemed alert and responsive, though sometimes slow to answer. He rightly corrected his attorney once—"a psychiatrist *is* a doctor," he said admonishingly. The defendant appeared patient and seemed to handle the stress of testifying quite well.

He did appear to show the influence of the various attorneys and psychiatrists with whom he had spent so much time; he freely and accurately used psychiatric and legal jargon like "delusional" and "psychotic."

Chase's account of what had happened between the time he purchased the .22 and the Miroth murders was sketchy. He remembered driving around shooting his new gun but did not think he saw Ambrose Griffin at the time of his murder. He remembered talking to his former classmate Nancy Holden just before he shot Teresa Wallin.

The defendant said he had been wandering around, "semiconscious" when he shot Wallin. Some things about the murder he remembered, but other things he claimed not to recall. He did admit to drinking some of Teresa's blood.

Chase said that after several days in a "blackout," on the morning of the twenty-seventh he drove to the Country Club Centre and parked. He had intended to shoot an old friend who he thought had become a political revolutionary and intended to kill him. But instead he went into his house and shot some other people.

He denied sodomizing Evelyn Miroth (a pathologist had testified to his findings), or even of removing her clothes. He thought it *was* possible he had cut her open and smeared blood on her body, but he couldn't remember "for sure."

Chase openly admitted to shooting little David Ferreira. At the time, he said, he thought the baby was something else, but he did not say what. He decapitated the child, he said, to get its blood and left with the baby in a green bucket, intending to drink more of its blood.

He had, he explained, started drinking blood after watching some "medical shows" on TV. He started with rabbit and bird blood, then dogs, cows, and finally humans.

He finished his testimony by claiming to have been victimized by society. His trouble, he stated, could be traced back to his inability to have successful, normal sex relations with his girlfriends.

Was he sorry for the murders? his attorney asked.

"Yes," Chase replied casually.

Ron Tochterman, in summation, covered Chase's protracted consideration before killing, nailing down premeditation, a required element of first-degree murder.

Then he walked the jury through the defendant's purchase of the .22 handgun and showed how his "violence escalated" from killing animals to shooting at people in their houses to murdering the man standing on his own lawn.

He covered the various neighborhood burglaries, going over the description of the suspect, which so fit Chase, and the Nancy Holden chance encounter.

And in chilling detail he recounted the crimes, which he labeled "sheer sexual sadism motivated by a literal blood lust." Throughout his discourse he showed time and again how Chase had understood that he was committing a crime, and how he strived to avoid detection.

"Teresa Wallin's body was dragged down the hallway of her home," the prosecutor said, "to get it out of sight. He had with him the rubber gloves which he would use when he got and drank blood from Mrs. Wallin's body." He had brought these with him, anticipating the killing—the gloves did *not* belong to the Wallins.

"He cut her open. He carefully mutilated internal organs. These were not wild, unaimed slashes. Particular organs were purposefully attacked. This was done in such a way that there was no incidental cutting of the intestines. He drank her blood, using a yogurt container which he apparently got from a garbage bag Mrs. Wallin had been carrying when she was killed.

"After finishing with Mrs. Wallin's body he washed the blood off his hands in the bathroom, washed the blood from the knife, and placed the knife in a rack of dishes in the kitchen, further evidence he knew what he was doing. He did not want to be seen, so he left by the back door."

Tochterman reminded the jury that Chase had told a psychiatrist he then went home and waited for the newspaper to come the next morning so he could read about the Wallin killing.

During the next four days, before the Miroth killings, Chase was "casing her neighborhood," knocking on doors on the pretext of collecting old magazines, the jury was told.

While there were lapses in Chase's judgment—he parked his car in a conspicuous no-parking zone of the Country Club Centre, for example—Tochterman said the defendant exhibited the same kind of planning in the murder of four persons at the Miroth home on January 27, 1978.

The prosecutor was not about to let on with the jury. He wanted them to be reminded of *every* horrible act.

"Again, he brought rubber gloves, which he would use when he got and drank blood from Mrs. Miroth's body.

"Between 10 A.M. and 11:15 A.M. Mr. Chase entered the Miroth residence and killed everyone inside. He shot Daniel Meredith twice in the head in the living room. He shot him once apparently while he was standing, then a second time as he lay face up on the floor to make sure he was dead. He shot six-year-old Jason Miroth once through the back of the neck and once through the head. Jason was shot in the living room, and his body was moved to the front bedroom floor.

"Mr. Chase exhibited deliberate caution in moving the bodies of Meredith and young Jason out of view from the front picture window to the bedroom.

"Evelyn Miroth was shot once in the head. She was stripped naked. Mr. Chase cut open her abdomen with two distinct, crossing cuts. He carefully attacked particular internal organs. The liver was cut, the tissues supporting the abdomen were torn, and the back of the abdomen was cut. No incidental damage to intestines was inflicted. Some of Mrs. Miroth's clothes were found in the bathroom. There was bloody water in the bathroom. Mrs. Miroth had knife wounds in the rectal area, two cuts through the anal area and the rectal wall, and six stab marks in the uterine wall. The knife was apparently thrust back and forth in the wound. Mr. Chase sodomized Mrs. Miroth's body, achieving orgasm.

"Mr. Chase carefully enucleated Mrs. Miroth's right eye. This involved precise, careful cutting.

"Mr. Chase shot David Ferreira in the head in his crib. He opened up the back of David's skull with a knife. Part of the baby's brain was found in the bathtub."

He left with the baby's body after a neighbor knocked on the door, the prosecutor continued. "He had the presence of mind and self-control to stop his activities and effect a getaway undetected. He had the presence of mind to take Mr. Meredith's car rather than try to get to his own vehicle, which was close by.

"Mr. Chase got back to his apartment and got the baby's body inside without being seen. He got rid of Mr. Meredith's car, leaving it locked and parked in the parking lot of the Sandpiper Apartments, the west boundary of which bordered on the east boundary of Mr. Chase's apartment complex. He obviously was aware he had to move fast to cover his tracks—with people checking for the Miroths, the crimes would soon be discovered. He had to get his Ranchero out of the area. He returned to Country Club Centre and got his car. It was gone by 12:15 P.M. that day."

"Mr. Chase further mutilated David Ferrerira's body at his apartment. More pieces of brain were found there. When eventually found, the body showed a gunshot wound to the head, and stab and incised wounds to the back of the skull. The largest opening was two and one half inches long. There was a gaping wound to the chest and abdomen; ribs three through ten were broken. The buttocks had been stabbed, and there was a cutting wound from the rectum to the sacrum. The body was decapitated.

"Mr. Chase understood he had to dispose of the body and evidence which would incriminate him. He had or obtained two large empty cardboard boxes. He put the baby, the baby's clothes, and the keys to Mr. Meredith's car in one box. He took that box to a location about three quarters mile north of his apartment, where he dumped it over a fence enclosing a small, little-used area between the back of a church office and the rear of a market. It was found there with

the baby's badly decomposed and partially mummified body on March 24, 1978."

At the defense table Richard Chase showed no
emotion or reaction of any kind. In fact, he looked
bored, with his sunken, opaque eyes having a luster-
less quality. His weight had dropped to 107 pounds,
with scarcely an ounce of flesh clinging to his scare-
crow frame. (His jailers filed reports stating he would
go days without touching even a morsel of food. They
had also reported that Chase at times lasciviously
joked about having women brought to his cell.)

Defense attorney Farris Salamy, in his summation,
asked the jury to return verdicts of second-degree
murder rather than first-degree, a determination that
would save his client from receiving the death sentence.

"I just feel that to try to tell you that there is
something less than murder here is not a reasonable
way to argue to you," Salamy admitted.

His argument seemed surprising, given Chase's
pleas of not guilty and not guilty by reason of insanity
to the six counts of murder.

But in the interim there had been much conflicting
testimony by psychiatrists on Chase's state of mind at
the time of the slayings. Two defense psychiatrists
concluded Chase was legally insane at the time
(though in his cross-examination Tochterman more or
less took them both apart), and three prosecution
psychiatrists testified that he was *not* insane.

In light of the different opinions by the doctors,
Salamy asked the jurors to "take the bull by the
horns" and draw their own conclusions.

He argued that there were numerous times over the

past ten years, as Chase's mental condition deteriorated, at which something could have been done to treat his condition. But he had not gotten such help.

Tochterman, in his final words to the jury, eloquently argued that Chase was a sexual sadist who could only achieve sexual satisfaction when he maimed his two women victims. While acknowledging Chase "had and has" mental problems, the prosecutor contended the defendant had enough "knowing shrewdness" at the time to plan the killings and his getaways.

He asked the predominantly young eight-woman, four-man panel to convict Chase of six counts of first-degree murder.

In the end, the well-prepared prosecution team, the overwhelming physical evidence, and Chase's own words from the witness stand sealed the defendant's fate.

On May 8, 1979, after slightly more than five hours of deliberations following the four-month trial, the jury found Chase guilty of first-degree murder in the deaths of:

Ambrose Griffin
Teresa Wallin
Evelyn Miroth
Jason Miroth
Daniel Meredith
and David Ferreira

Six names I will remember as long as I live.

Six days later the sanity phase of his trial started with the same jury.

There was a rehash of the psychiatric testimony, after which Tochterman argued that Chase was not so mentally ill that he could not conform his conduct to the requirements of the law.

After deliberating only sixty-five minutes the jury found Chase legally sane, paving the way for the third and final phase of the trial: the penalty phase.

Would Chase receive life in prison without possibility of parole, or the death sentence?

On May 16 Chase again took the stand, facing the same jury that had convicted him of murder and found him sane.

"I beg for another chance to survive," he said. "I hope to make compensation for the families. I am a good person, although weak in heart and mind."

When it was Tochterman's turn he described Chase as a "monster" who since adolescence had exhibited a "pattern of gross selfishness and gross callousness.

"If Mr. Chase truly believed he needed blood [to survive], that in no way mitigates his culpability in committing the killings. The fact that a person kills for perverse or bizarre reasons cannot be taken as a mitigating circumstance."

The prosecutor said Chase's life was not "salvageable. I submit that you have to be the most naïve optimist, a Pollyanna ten times over, to believe that Mr. Chase has the possibility to be a decent human being. He is a dangerous person, he is a time bomb."

In closing Tochterman suggested, tight-lipped, that if the jurors wanted to give Chase a break, "I would suggest that the break he is entitled to is the same break he gave to his victims Teresa Wallin, David

Ferreira, Jason Miroth, Daniel Meredith, Evelyn Miroth, and Ambrose Griffin."

The next day, after just more than four hours of deliberations, the jury sentenced Richard Chase to die in the lethal gas chamber at San Quentin Penitentiary.

By some strange twist of fate—supporting, I suppose, that religious phrase we hear so often at funerals, "the Lord giveth and the Lord taketh away"—Tochterman's assistant, Al Locher, left court and went directly to a Sacramento-area hospital, where his wife gave birth that very day to a healthy baby boy.

16

December 26, 1980

Christmas had come and gone without much celebration at San Quentin Penitentiary, nestled along the upper shores of San Francisco Bay at the western base of the Richmond–San Rafael Bridge.

The prison, huddled next to an inhospitable stretch of beach, is a complex of cheerless and unrepentant buildings; together they form the oldest, most unattractive landmark on the north edge of the bay.

Several thousand medium-security prisoners of the State of California live there. Also, housed in single cells in a prison within the prison, are the few hundred maximum-security inmates who live on Death Row. Isolated from the rest of the prison population, the men on Death Row wait to share their fate with the prisoners who lived there for a while in less complicated and considerably less tolerant days before heading into the gas chamber. Of course, every one of these Death Row residents lived with a dream: that the frivolous California voters would change their minds one more time about the death penalty, and their sentences would be commuted to life.

At 8:15 this morning a correctional officer assigned to guard duty on Death Row greeted the prisoner in Cell 5800 with as much good cheer as the occasion demanded, which was not much.

Christmas was gone, for what that was worth, and things would settle down to normal on Death Row, crowded now by several hundred men who had been condemned to die and who spent their lives trying to avoid the cyanide pellet scheduled one day to drop into a small tank of acid and end their waiting and wondering.

Richard Chase, the prisoner in 5800, was moody at best. Sometimes he answered the guard's greeting, other times he did not. He was lying on his back and breathing normally when the guard looked in his cell.

Less than three hours later, at 11:05 A.M., the same guard checked Chase's cell again. The prisoner was lying on his stomach with both legs extended off his bunk and his feet on the floor. His head was turned into the mattress and his arms extended upward, into the pillow.

The guard knew this inmate liked to sleep with a pillow over his head, as if blocking out the world around him. But this didn't look right.

After calling the prisoner's name and waiting for a few moments, the guard realized the prisoner was not breathing. He opened the cell door, pulled the prisoner from his cell, and, after determining that the prisoner was in fact dead, left him lying on his back.

The Marin County Coroner's Office was called.

When coroner investigator K. P. Holmes arrived he glanced cursorily at the body, then entered the cell and examined it. He found small amounts of blood soaked into the bedsheet where the inmate's head had been lying.

Some cardboard boxes were found next to the bed, and in them were four sheets of letter-sized paper covered with handwriting. Two pages contained some sort of a graph, the squares filled with some sort of cryptographic code. The other two pages contained the strangest sort of suicide note. It was a rambling message in which the inmate warned that he might take some pills and that his heart might stop beating as a result.

Some pills were available. It was learned that the prison physician had prescribed for Chase three daily fifty-milligram tablets of Sinequan (doxepin hydrochloride), a psychotherapeutic agent given for depression. The strength of the medication fell well within the normal dose. In prison inmates are only given a daily dose of their medication, never enough for purposeful overdoses.

Pathologists who autopsied the body diagnosed the cause of death as toxic ingestion. They also found the heart that its owner had worried so much about "of normal size, the coronary arterial tree free of sclerosis," and all valves in good shape.

Lab reports confirmed the cause of death. As measured in a urine sample drawn from the corpse, the level of doxepin in Chase's body exceeded the therapeutic range by thirty-six times—and was exactly twelve times greater than the drug's toxic level.

The "daily packet" of Chase's antidepressant drug

was found untouched in his cell, suggesting that he had saved his daily pills for possibly as long as two or three weeks before ingesting them that morning.

Chase's prison psychiatrist was interviewed by the coroner's office. For the record, the physician stated that his patient was "very psychotic and had been since his arrival at San Quentin." He had been transferred to Vacaville Mental Facility for four months earlier in 1980 and had been brought back to San Quentin in April.

The psychiatrist remembered something else about his patient. "His crimes were committed around the Christmas holidays three years ago," the physician reported. "There might well have been an anniversary phenomenon involved in the timing of his suicide."

Richard Chase died exactly one day short of three years after the Miroth killings.

When I heard of his suicide in prison I thought it rather odd. I honestly didn't think our East Side Killer was suicidal. But I did note the irony in the way in which he died: Richard Chase ended up being poisoned to death, all right—by his own hand.

With the ever-changing political climate in the state, I hadn't been sure if he would actually be put to death in the gas chamber.

Now, frankly, I was just relieved he was gone.

Also available from Mondo

THE MAN WHO COULD NOT KILL ENOUGH
The Secret Murders of Jeffrey Dahmer

Anne E. Schwartz

An astounding midnight phone call from a Milwaukee police contact was to give local crime reporter Anne Schwartz the scoop of a lifetime: first-hand involvement from the start in the horrifying case of the cannibal serial killer, Jeffrey Dahmer.

From her own direct experience, Schwartz here tells the whole story - from the gruesome discovery of human remains in Dahmer's apartment, through the course of the police investigation, to the trial and eventual sentencing of Dahmer to fifteen life terms.

She has gained the confidence of the victims' families and exclusive access to the police, attorneys and judges involved. Crucially, she has looked into Dahmer's past to try to answer two crucial questions: why did he kill, and why was he not stopped earlier?

For a complete list of Mondo publications and the opportunity to buy this exclusive Mondo T-shirt, please send a large SAE to:
Mondo Mail Order, 19 Valentine Place, London SE1 8QH.
Please quote reference MB4.